Institution Building in Urban Education

Institution Building in Urban Education

by Morris Janowitz, *University of Chicago*

RUSSELL SAGE FOUNDATION • 1969

PUBLICATIONS OF RUSSELL SAGE FOUNDATION

Russell Sage Foundation was established in 1907 by Mrs. Russell Sage for the improvement of social and living conditions in the United States. In carrying out its purpose the Foundation conducts research under the direction of members of the staff or in close collaboration with other institutions, and supports programs designed to develop and demonstrate productive working relations between social scientists and other professional groups. As an integral part of its operations, the Foundation from time to time publishes books or pamphlets resulting from these activities. Publication under the imprint of the Foundation does not necessarily imply agreement by the Foundation, its Trustees, or its staff with the interpretations or conclusions of the authors.

© *1969 by Russell Sage Foundation*
Printed in the United States of America by
Connecticut Printers, Inc., Hartford, Connecticut

Library of Congress Catalog Card Number: 72-81407

Contents

v

Preface

In preparing this volume, I have tried to present a sociological perspective on the issues involved in transforming the institutional structure of inner city schools. My concern has been with closing the gap between sociological analysis and public policy, and professional practice and citizen participation. My orientation is that this gap will not be closed by seeking to develop an "action" sociology. Instead, there is need for critical analysis of alternative strategies and approaches which draws on social science concepts and findings. There is need for effective research on the process of social change in public education. The validity and relevance of my hypotheses will have to be tested by the experiences of the new breed of school administrators who are prepared to be self-critical about their tasks and to collect meaningful data.

I have drawn on published and unpublished studies of experimental programs in urban education, and on various surveys and proposals for reorganizing public school systems. I have sought to include conclusions drawn from the experiences of a variety of experts, especially curriculum development specialists and entrepreneurs of automated and electronic teaching equipment. The concepts used in this volume are derived from the research program on urban education of the Center for Social Organization Studies, which has been organized by David Street and his collaborators and generously supported by the Russell Sage Foundation.

This study also encompasses my personal experiences with educational research and development programs since 1961, which range from small-scale volunteer tutoring programs to comprehensive experimental inner city school districts under the Delinquency Control Act and more recently under the Model Cities Program. My experiences include involvement in the South Commons development on the Near South side of Chicago, which seeks to integrate urban renewal planning with the activities of the Board of Education. It draws heavily on the materials collected by Gayle Janowitz in her demonstration work on volunteers in education and reported in "After School Study Centers: Experimental Materials and Clinical Research." The policy implications of these efforts were stated in a report to the Superintendent of the Board of Education of the City of Chicago, "Innovation in the Public School System of the Inner City: A Policy Perspective," Working Paper No. 48, Center for Social Organization Studies, June, 1965. A thoughtful summary of the organizational difficulties of innovation in public education, based on these materials, was published by Nicholas von Hoffman in the *Washington Post,* January 15, 1967.

I wish to acknowledge the critical interest of Orville G. Brim, Jr., which has led me toward a more systematic approach to institution building in public education.

University of Chicago   MORRIS JANOWITZ
October 1, 1968

1. The Slum School
and Contemporary Society

By the middle of the 1960's sociological categories had come to pervade popular and professional thinking about slum schools and education of the lower class. Militant demands for improving the effectiveness of inner city education have incorporated the rhetoric of sociology because of the realities of social class and race. Terms such as "cultural deprivation" and "deviant behavior" were no longer technical jargon but the language of political debate. The persistent criticism of intelligence and psychological testing and the growth of awareness of the social and cultural problems of the slum school facilitated a rapid introduction of sociological analysis into policy issues.

There has been a long tradition that the more the teacher knows about the psychology of the pupils, the more effective the school system would be. It was inevitable that the first steps in the application of the sociology of education would focus on empirical findings about the social and cultural characteristics of the student body. In turn, educators have developed an interest in the social characteristics of the pupils of the inner city. If such inquiry and discussion is pursued in a sympathetic and detached fashion, it would be difficult to argue against this perspective. The introduction of special courses on the culturally deprived and manuals on the social characteristics of inner city children frequently, however, degenerate into a search for another set of schematic principles for imposing order on an intractable social environment.

A second step in the utilization of sociological findings has been in the preparation of curricular materials for the inner city. Obviously, to know more about the social environment of the school is an aid in the preparation of teaching materials. The sociology of education can be disruptive, however, if it leads to the development of a specialized and distinctly separate curriculum which is designed to meet the needs of low income children. The teacher who stresses the human differences between lower-class and middle-class pupils, rather than their similarities, is certain to complicate his professional tasks and to contribute further to social separateness.

Fortunately, the sociological contribution to educational policy and practice has broadened to include a concern with the school as a social institution, that is, as a social system. The terms "social institution" and "social system" can be used interchangeably, although social system is coming to replace the older term, social institution. I prefer not to lose sight completely of the concept social institution, because for me it includes a more concrete dimension. To think of the school, especially the slum school, as a social institution is to encompass its empirical realities, such as the physical structure, the community setting, and the human beings involved, as well as the persistent patterns of behavior. The tasks of this book are to explore the basic characteristics of the school as a social institution and to determine the relevance of sociological categories for institution building in education; that is, for transforming it and adapting it to meet contemporary requirements.

"PEOPLE CHANGING" INSTITUTIONS

The problems of institution building for inner city schools are not unique. There is, strangely enough, a powerful analogy between the mental hospital or the correctional institution and the slum school. It makes a great deal of sense for sociologists to refer to them as "people changing" institutions.[1] The school has been assigned the task of socializing or resocializing the motives and values of its pupils, in a manner comparable to the mental hospital or the correctional institution. Ideally, the school in the lower-class community should supply a link by which youngsters are able to enter the mainstream of American society.

During the last two decades, sociological analysis has played a creative role in efforts to transform the goals of mental hospitals and juvenile correctional institutions from "custody" to "treatment." Once the goal of sheer custody was abandoned, the contribution of sociological thinking was conceptual. It assisted in broadening professional practice from a limited concern with restructuring individual motives to the development and management of a more meaningful institution with goals of treatment or rehabilitation. The term "organization milieu" or "climate" has come to refer to the total setting of a "people changing" institution.

As a result, there has developed a body of research literature on "people changing" institutions and a common language of discourse between social investigators and selected administrators. Of course, it is an open question whether in terms of quantitative measures of performance these transformations have drastically improved the "efficiency" of such institutions. It is clear, however, that the social and moral climate of mental hospitals or training schools can be altered to become more compatible with the standards of a humane society that stresses self-respect and dignity.

Clearly, progress in the mental health field has in part been the result of a broad political and social movement propelled by humanitarian impulses. Nevertheless, the social sciences and sociol-

[1] See David Street, Robert Vinter, and Charles Perrow, *Organization for Treatment* (New York: Free Press, 1966).

ogy, in particular, have made a contribution in helping to clarify the requirements for an appropriate milieu. Empirical research on "people changing" institutions has helped to identify the organizational variables that make possible more rational and more effective management of such institutions.

To acknowledge developments in mental health, for example, does not require an overstatement of the extent to which goals have been achieved in transforming the organizational format of the mental hospital. The number of institutions that approximate ideal standards remains very limited indeed. The milieu of the average institution has been improved in the last decade, however, and the concentration of strongly repressive ones has declined. Nevertheless, the essential issue at hand is the availability of a conceptual model—an holistic and integrated one at that— that offers a goal for professionals and policy makers.

A custodial institution is one in which the relations between staff and clients are based on mutual mistrust and hostility. In many crucial respects, the slum school has such a character. But it has not had a transformation parallel to that of the mental hospital or correctional institution, either in organizational concepts or in effective administration and professional practice. This is a strange paradox because the schools are a much more vital institution to society than are the mental hospitals or the correctional institutions. It is also strange because one would have assumed that it would be more feasible to adapt and creatively improve the school with its much younger and more malleable student body. It would seem harder to deal with problems of the mental hospital or the correctional institution whose clients may have deeply fixed personality structures and patterns of deviant behavior.

By any measure, the amount of progress in inner city schools during the last twenty years of social ferment is not impressive. In fact, our argument is partly based on the assumption that the level of performance relative to new societal demands on public education is not comparable to the development of the organizational milieu or organizational climate in the mental hospital. Socal science researchers, and especially sociologists, have not developed a similar common discourse with school administrators which would contribute to more effective management of inner city schools.

It needs to be emphasized that the absence of strategic models of change which see the school as a social institution is due in part to the fact that the administrators have been operating with limited resources. They have developed such strong defensive postures that they are inhibited in formulating new strategic conceptions. A whole generation of top-level administrators seems destined to be retired or circumvented rather than to lead a professional reorientation. The successful big-city superintendent is the man who can in advance bargain for the conditions to eliminate the old guard.

In part, we are also dealing with the absence of an effective intellectual and research tradition about school administration. The present state of writing about educational administration, despite the large number of available books, offers little special stimulus. Since the 1950's, graduate schools of education have concerned themselves with the intellectual basis of the profession. The approach has been to infuse social sciences into their training. The quality of educational administrators in training has increased markedly, and a new generation is entering the middle ranks. There exist some highly relevant treatises on educational administration, as for example, Campbell, Corbally, and Ramseyer, but this is not an extensive and adequate body of scholarly or research literature.[2]

[2] Roald F. Campbell, John E. Corbally, Jr., and John A. Ramseyer, *Introduction to Educational Administration* (Boston: Allyn and Bacon, 1966).

This absence of an effective body of literature on educational institutions has been repeatedly noted by research scholars. In 1956, Neal Gross reported that there was no systematic study of school organization.[3] A decade later, Charles E. Bidwell concluded his comprehensive review of the organizational research literature with the same pronouncement.[4] One can still point to Willard Waller's *The Sociology of Teaching,* published in 1932, as a pioneer classic that has remarkably enduring value because of its realism and vivid insights.[5] More recent analytic writings have included contributions by Jacob W. Getzels, Fred E. Katz, and Talcott Parsons.[6]

Perhaps one of the most pointed observations that can be made about the literature of educational institutions is the absence of autobiographical materials by administrators, in contrast to revealing documents produced by businessmen, and by political and military leaders. Although it is a verbal and literate profession, educational administration has not developed a sense of self-reflection.

From an intellectual point of view, clearly a first step in developing models of change—although only a first step—is greater

[3] Neal Gross, "Sociology of Education, 1945–1955," in Hans T. Zetterberg (ed.), *Sociology in the United States: A Trend Report* (Paris: UNESCO, 1956), 62–67.

[4] Charles E. Bidwell, "The School as a Formal Organization," in James G. March (ed.), *Handbook of Organizations* (Chicago: Rand McNally & Company, 1965).

[5] Willard Waller, *The Sociology of Teaching* (New York: John Wiley & Sons, 1932).

[6] Jacob W. Getzels, "A Psycho-sociological Framework for the Study of Educational Administration," *Harvard Educational Review,* 22 (1952), 235–246; Talcott Parsons, "The School Class as a Social System: Some of Its Functions in American Society." *Harvard Educational Review,* 29 (1959), 297–318; Fred E. Katz, "The School as a Complex Social Organization," *Harvard Educational Review,* 34 (1964), 428–455.

agreement on the sources of the present "crisis" in inner city public education.

THE "CRISIS" IN EDUCATION

It is possible to distinguish between an "old crisis" and a "new crisis" in public education. In other words, to evaluate the school crisis in the inner city, it is necessary to separate contemporary issues from those which have persisted over the last half century.

To speak of the "old crisis" in public education is not only to draw attention to the traditional inferiority and ineffectiveness of Negro schools, but also to other long-standing pockets of inadequate education in older working-class communities serving selected second- and third-generation European immigrants, or southern White Appalachian families, or chronically depressed rural areas. The "old crisis" is the persistence of gross inequalities in educational resources which derive from the local organizational format of public education and the absence of minimum national standards. If the traditions of American public education have been adapted to the social, cultural, regional, and religious diversity of the United States, this advantage has been purchased at the cost of highly uneven minimum performance.

In addition to unequal economic expenditures, the educational crisis for the Negro student has its cultural and psychological dimensions. Race prejudice has made the experience of the Negro in the public school system different from that of other minority and immigrant groups. In this sense the crisis is an old one. Already in the 1930's, as a result of the work of E. Franklin Frazier, sociologists pointed to the profound disarticulation between educational institutions and the social organization and culture of the Negro family, which was fashioned by slavery and by post-emancipation segregation. Negro schools, both in the North and in the South, were traditionally inferior. Until about 1960, professional educators did not show impressive initiative in seeking to deal with these problems.

The inequality of educational opportunities has persisted during a period of long-term growth in effectiveness of the system, which only served to deepen the tensions created by these irregularities. For the nation as a whole, the retention rate of youngsters in high school has risen continually in recent decades. For example, out of every 1,000 pupils who entered the fifth grade in 1945, 525 later graduated from high school. By 1957, 710 fifth graders out of every 1,000 were eventually able to graduate from high school. The figure continues to rise; of every 1,000 fifth graders in 1965, it is estimated that approximately 800 will ultimately graduate from high school. This expansion in retention rates is not merely a custodial enterprise, for results of achievement tests suggest that the levels of overall academic performance of elementary and secondary school populations have risen during the last two decades. Of particular note has been the sharp upgrading of college preparatory programs in the United States to the point where an important minority of high schools offer first- and second-year college level work. (These increased standards of academic performance in secondary education had reached the point in the mid-1960's where educators were questioning whether high school students had the emotional maturity to comprehend, in meaningful terms, parts of the improved curriculum. Mental health specialists were also concerned with the emotional impact of high school social climates in which new academic standards narrowed the basis for personal and social maturity.)

The "new crisis" in public education is linked to a different set of factors, namely, the transformation and organization of the labor market under advanced industrialization. In the past, at least up to the Great Depression, the socialization of youngsters from European immigrant families and of migrants from rural areas was in good measure accomplished through work experiences—part time and full time. This is not to overlook the fact that the comprehensive high school served as a powerful mechanism in stimulating students from low-income families to acquire academic skills and social orientations required for college education. Since 1945 in the United States, high school graduation or its equivalent—not only in terms of academic and vocational requirements, but also in terms of social attitude, interpersonal competence, and maturity—is defined as a desirable and required goal, even for the lowest income groups. No society has ever exposed its lower class to such a process of socialization and to such opportunities. The public school system never had to cope with such societal demands. Actual work requirements, changed standards of employment and trade unions, and new legislation about minimum wages account for this transformation. Public educators have been prepared to follow these trends and to extend high school education as a desirable goal per se. Therefore, it makes little sense to speak of a decrease in the effectiveness of the high school system in catering to the needs of lower-class youths. The inner city high school has been weakened and, in this sense, there has been an actual deterioration of the quality of available public education. Nevertheless, the "crisis" in education is a "new crisis" because schools must now accept responsibility for all youngsters who are not college bound until they develop levels of personal maturity sufficient for them to enter the labor market. The present resources and practices of the inner city school system are inadequate for this expanded task.

These trends have special relevance for Negro students, who are concentrated in the inner city and are particularly vulnerable to the impact of technological changes in the labor market. It is well known that these technological changes are complicating the process of assimilating the Negro into the mainstream of society.

Those jobs in the semi-skilled category which in an earlier period supplied the major opportunity for other minorities to enter the labor market and become socialized into the larger society are declining. Access to these semi-skilled jobs is also complicated for Negroes by residential location and transportation.

Thus, the "old crisis" and the "new crisis" fuse as low-income and Negro populations concentrate in the older central cities. But institution building in public education confronts not only the issues of equality of opportunity (the extension of the "old crisis"), but also the formulation of new practices (the consequence of the "new crisis").

EFFORTS AT SEGMENTAL CHANGE

As a means of dealing with the "old" and the "new crisis," innovation in the inner city schools has been highly fragmentary. A decade of vigorous intellectual criticism from 1955 to 1965, plus extensive professional and experimental efforts, did not produce educational developments in the inner city that satisfied the demands of public pressure. Nor were sensitive professionals satisfied with the rate of progress.

Leading experts have been concerned with specific practical problems or particular aspects of school administration. There has been considerable inventive thinking about the pacing of the classroom curriculum, namely in development of various schemes of nongrading, multigrading, or continuous education. Vast efforts have been undertaken in developing administrative schemes for achieving racial integration both of teachers and of pupils. There have been various formulations of new roles in public education ranging from the master teacher to the school-community agent. But all of these approaches must be considered to be partial models of transformation, especially in contrast to the comprehensive and holistic concepts and schemes that have been developed for other "people changing" institutions.

One of the rare efforts at comprehensive reformulation of inner city education is found in the writings of Robert J. Havighurst.[7] The importance of his approach rests in the fact that he directly approached the policy issues of both social class and racial segregation in urban education. He placed high emphasis on achieving racial integration, thereby seeking to continue what he believed to be our tradition of social heterogeneity. But in the contemporary context of metropolitan urbanism, he is prepared to trade off social-class heterogeneity for progress in racial integration. He is fully aware that integration is most likely to be achieved in middle-class groups.

The core of Havighurst's framework for restructuring the inner city public school system is organizational and not interpersonal. In his view, the metropolitan public school system needs to be reorganized into larger organizational units, four or five super units at most. In each unit there should be an appropriate racial balance insuring managed integration, but each educational sector should have a distinctive social-class composition and an educational program to serve the needs of its student population. The comprehensive high school gives way to a greater degree of educational specialization along socioeconomic lines.

Havighurst is seeking a comprehensive restructuring of public education in the inner city. He believes that he is continuing the pragmatic tradition of American education. A public presentation of his approach and the operational plan for implementing it were offered in his survey of the Chicago public school system in 1964.[8] The Chicago public school system was then under the direction of Benjamin Willis and there was widespread public discontent with its management. As an expression of their authority, the members of the Board of Education commissioned Havighurst

[7] See especially Robert J. Havighurst, *The Public Schools of Chicago: A Survey* (Chicago: Board of Education of the City of Chicago, 1964).
[8] *Ibid.*

to make a survey and produce a set of recommendations. Neither Benjamin Willis, the members of the school board, nor the key citizen groups concerned with innovation endorsed or accepted his basic notions. Although Havighurst's ideas have been widely disseminated throughout the United States, there has not been a single case in which this set of proposals has been adopted by a major public education system.

In the absence of an appropriate concept for strategic innovation, efforts to improve the effectiveness of inner city school systems can best be described as segmental change. The reforms in public education since the end of World War II started with a concern for increasing the quality of high school education for college bound students. In part it was the result of new definitions of education for scientific and educational careers; in part it was a reflection of a social structure that was making education a more and more important criteria for social mobility; and in part it was a response to competition with the Soviet Union.

This trend can be called the "Europeanization" of American public education. It represented partly the efforts of university professors who advocated the improvement of American society politically and culturally by training youngsters both earlier and more thoroughly in basic disciplines. The drive for Europeanization of the secondary school was being developed during a period when, paradoxically, social democratic governments of Western Europe were struggling to introduce the American comprehensive high school in an effort to modernize their social structure.

The impetus of academic reform in the United States led to elaborate curriculum reform efforts, not to changing the organizational format. The result may well have been to weaken the comprehensive high school system as it forced the decision to prepare for college, especially for entrance to a superior college, to an earlier age. This is not to deny that the curriculum reform movement brought a select number of high schools back to higher levels of academic performance such as existed in 1920 and 1930, when many competent adults entered high school teaching only because of the absence of college-level teaching opportunities.

After 1960, the goals of reform in public education were transformed by the civil rights movement, and by political pressures to reduce poverty. The focus shifted to the slum school. The economic and fiscal context has become well known. Discrepancies in the level of educational expenditures and the quality of public education in the inner city versus the suburbs have become so well known as to generate profound political tensions.[9] Because of the superior political position of rural and suburban areas, the allocation of state aid has tended to work against the inner city. Moreover, suburban areas have their socioeconomic position enhanced by the services rendered to them by the central city. Thus, for example, it has been estimated that for some metropolitan areas expenditures for central city education could be raised by at least fifty dollars per pupil if the full cost the central city residents pay for services rendered to suburban residents employed in the central city were returned to the city.

The financial problems of inner city public school systems have been made more difficult by the pattern of Federal aid to education. Until 1965, as a result of explicit political decisions by Congress, Federal aid was almost exclusively directed to the support of higher education, rather than to primary or secondary levels. The first efforts at Federal aid to secondary education in the inner city were proposed not by a liberal, but by a conservative, Senator Robert Taft of Ohio, in 1948. But Congress refused to act because of tensions and conflicts over aid to religious schools. Support for higher education was more feasible since the con-

[9] "The Rich Get Richer the Poor Get Poorer . . . Schools," *Carnegie Quarterly,* Vol. 14, No. 4 (Fall, 1966), pp. 1–3.

tending parties were less divided. The result of the emphasis on higher education meant greater benefits to middle-class and suburban families rather than to lower-class or central city families.

Since 1965, expenditures for Federal aid to primary and secondary school education have been growing with some priority to inner city requirements, but they have not been of a magnitude to cause fundamental reallocation of public expenditures required to close the gap between the suburbs and the central city. Moreover, changes in Federal allocations must be balanced against the willingness of state legislatures to give high priority and allocate extensive sums of money to higher education at the expense of increased state aid to the inner city. Again, these expenditures on higher education disproportionately benefit higher-income and suburban families. It has been carefully documented that even the curriculum development programs, financed by the Federal government, have disproportionately benefited the suburban and the upper socioeconomic communities.[10]

A dramatic but typical example can be seen in the construction of the University of Illinois Chicago Circle campus, a state university which was designed for the urban community and which was symbolically located in the heart of the inner city, but which in effect draws its student body heavily from the surrounding suburban areas. During the period 1960–1965, while the Chicago Board of Education had extremely limited funds for essential high school construction, the State of Illinois invested almost half a billion dollars in the University of Illinois Chicago Circle campus. As of 1965, only about 3 per cent of the University of Illinois Chicago Circle Campus students were Negro, and the prospect of more than limited increase during the subsequent five-year period

[10] Roald F. Campbell and Robert A. Bunnell, "Differential Impact of National Programs on Secondary Schools," *The School Review*, 71, No. 4 (1963), 464–476.

remains very remote. Political pressures generated by this experience have led the administrators of the University of Illinois system to propose a second "specialized" university community west of the existing campus which would emphasize remedial college education.

As new funds have become available, inner city school systems in one fashion or another sought to develop new experimental programs. Initially, funds were made available by private groups and by specialized government legislation, such as the Delinquency Control Act of 1961, which sought on an experimental basis to stimulate integration of school programs with community agencies and organizations. The second stage began with the passage of various programs of the Office of Economic Opportunity and involved new but unstable allocations of funds for educational development. With the passage of the Elementary and Secondary School Act of 1965, there emerged a more permanent basis for institution building, since Federal funds were specifically designed to assist city school systems with immediate fiscal problems and to stimulate innovation. In addition, there were special funds available for experiments in desegregation plus a variety of other special purposes all of which had long-term implications for school development. In fact, it could be argued that the variety and complexity of Federal funds created a difficult and unwieldy administrative formula. Congressional leaders, however, initially believed that legislation should be drawn to stimulate innovation. In due course, Congress has moved away from such an approach to more blanket funding and a return to the support of state and local leadership. With the passage of the Model Cities Act in 1966, the Federal government again demonstrated interest in innovations that would link school programs with housing and social development. Nevertheless, the subsequent and rapid growth of Black Power movements in public education have meant that

educational innovation must often take place in a setting in which
the demands for participation and for group recognition have become extremely pronounced and immediate.

In a short period of time, by 1968, most school systems of the
United States had had some experience with these conscious efforts to improve the quality of their educational programs. Such
efforts ranged from such limited programs as new libraries to
"saturation" programs in selected schools.

Some students of slum life anticipated that mass education in
the inner city would have an institutional character that would
produce powerful resistance to change even when new resources
were made available. All available evidence has confirmed this
expectation. It is not easy to identify the real barriers to organizational innovation in public education. The typical suburban
school is part of a much smaller system. This dimension by itself
facilitates change in suburban schools. The sheer size of the central city school system becomes of overriding importance when
one considers the logistics of change. But clearly resistance to
change is more than a matter of organizational size, for large-
scale organizations do institute drastic and basic changes. Resistance to change is rooted in the basic decision-making and authority structure of the public school system.

First, these experiences in educational innovation seem to
underline the conclusion that the infusion of new funds into existing or only partially modified structures does not produce
higher levels of performance. Even significantly higher levels of
expenditure appear to have limited consequences. The per pupil
costs of education in New York City are the highest in the United
States, but there is no evidence that the level of performance is
discernibly higher. Of course, it can be argued that the measures
of performance are not precise or broad enough. It can also be
argued that the levels of expenditure in New York City are not
really high enough to make a crucial difference, or that the prob-

lems in New York City are more pressing and without these higher levels of expenditure the situation would be worse. Although these are relevant counter arguments, they do not reverse the basic contention that increased expenditures have not produced clearly discernible results.

This proposition can be highlighted by even a limited examination of the manner in which increased funds have been used. Aside from increased teacher salaries and higher operating costs for existing programs, the major thrust has been on the reduction of class size. This is true for most large metropolitan systems. In short, the basic response has been to continue the same procedures but on a more intensive basis. Such a response would be expected of an organization under pressure. In Chicago, Federal funds were actually used to increase the length of the school day. The educational procedures that produced a 40 per cent dropout rate and massive academic retardation by third grade were extended, with only minor modifications, for another hour. There exists a respectable body of literature that class size per se is unrelated to teaching effectiveness.[11] This is not to argue that there are no desirable upper limits in class size but rather to emphasize that limited reduction in class size without concomitant fundamental changes in classroom management is an uneconomic allocation of resources.

A great deal of thinking and research on the question of class size has come from the Swedish experience where governmental authorities have shown a continuing concern for improving the quality of education of low income groups. Sixten Marklund, in a 1962 report, stated the issue in the following terms:

> With regard to size, the most prevalent opinion is that a small class is more conducive to superior achievement. Explicitly or

[11] For a summary of this literature, see Neal Gross, "Memorandum on Class Size" (unpublished paper, August 15, 1961).

implicitly a reduced enrollment is justified on the grounds that pupils will do better scholastically. The term "achievement" is usually understood to refer both to level of knowledge and skills in academic subjects. This interpretation is embraced not only by teachers, who directly shoulder the heavy burden of large classes, but also by authorities, government commissions and groups of experts, and probably by parents and guardians as well.[12]

In summarizing the then existing data, he concluded that "the greater part of scientific research lends no support to this body of thinking."[13] On the basis of his extensive samples in Stockholm and throughout Sweden, he reaffirmed and further documented the same conclusion. Moreover, in addressing the question of whether classes should be made smaller, he concluded, "all we can say here is that a reduction, which can be defended on many grounds, will probably not lead to improved achievements unless steps are taken at the same time to utilize the enhanced peda-gogical opportunities which arise."[14] In other words, he sub-ordinates class size to "other and more essential factors."

In this connection it needs to be emphasized that teachers' unions in the United States have pressed hard for reduction in class size. The unionization movement is strongest in the large metropolitan areas where they have succeeded in some areas in reducing class size. Thus, it was reported for 1965 that in the 21 largest school districts with a population over 100,000 the median class size was 31.6.[15] These are the big city systems with the larg-

---

[12] Sixten Marklund, *Skolklassens Storlek och Struktur* (Scholastic Attain-ments as Related to Size and Homogeneity of Classes) (Stockholm: Alm-quist and Wiksell, 1962), 197.

[13] *Ibid.*

[14] *Ibid.*, 209.

[15] *National Education Association Research Bulletin*, Vol. 43, No. 4, December, 1965.

est Negro concentration. No doubt in these areas there is a somewhat larger class size in slum areas.

In the smaller school districts, however, class size is not much different. Thus, as the total enrollment of pupils in the districts declined, the median size of class hardly varied or declined only slightly. In the 749 districts with 6,000 to 11,000 pupils the median size dropped to 28.6 and for the 1,547 small districts with 5,000 students the median class size was 28.4. A similar pattern obtains for junior and senior high schools, indicating that gross inequalities in class size are being eliminated.

This discussion of size focuses on the number of youngsters in a classroom. There is, of course, another dimension of size, namely the size of a school building or a specific educational complex. At this level, as in any institutional enterprise, concern with optimum size is a highly important issue. In industrial enterprise, it has come to be recognized that there is an optimum size of a particular operating unit or of a cluster of units in an industrial division. In the case of the mental hospital and the correctional institution, it has been argued that there are also optimum sizes for effectiveness. The psychiatric profession has sought to establish standards as to the maximum size of mental hospitals, and there exists a body of research data to support these professional goals.[16] Even in the absence of adequate research, it is still most plausible that the notion of optimum size applies to educational institutions, both in terms of economic costs and for achieving appropriate organizational climate and milieu.

Second, Federal funds that have not been absorbed by higher teaching costs have been allocated for segmental change mainly in the form of demonstration projects rather than planning for fundamental institution building. The fate of demonstration projects, including large-scale projects, points to their inherent

[16] Leonard P. Ullman, *Institution and Outcome: A Comparative Study of Psychiatric Hospitals* (Oxford: Pergamon Press, 1967).

limitations. Widespread differences of professional opinion exist about the meaning and validity of specific criteria of success and failure as well as the adequacy of research design. There is little agreement about the scientific relevance of the findings of many demonstration projects. Often the "big factors" like the organizational setting of the school or the quality of leadership are left uncontrolled. As a result, research generated by demonstration projects frequently seems to focus on trivial variables. There is reason to believe that careful comparative analysis of operational records, including cost benefit analysis, will probably be as rewarding an approach as the evaluation of the limited demonstration project. The advantage of conducting research on demonstration projects flows from the detailed clinical and case-study analysis of teacher and student attitudes and reactions rather than from the quantitative data that are generated.

Moreover, the life history of most demonstration programs seems to be self-limiting. They have tended generally to be small scale and short lived, with professionals learning that results are not cumulative but rather seem to be disjunctive. There is a high turnover of personnel so that the consequences of a particular demonstration face gradual extinction. The most critical argument is that after a decision to spread the demonstration project throughout the system, it faces death by diffuse and partial incorporation. In addition, there is an absence of training to insure the implementation of new procedures, nor are there effective devices of inspection and audit. In the end, a considerable degree of frustration develops as old practices and procedures are given new names.

Although the bulk of the demonstration projects in public education are of limited scope and short duration, selected demonstration projects have grown in the amount of resources that are involved. The highly publicized and well-financed Higher Horizons demonstration project of the New York City Board of Education suffered the same fate as the typical small-scale demonstration enterprise. In a limited area effective work was undertaken in 1959. Higher Horizons sought to emphasize cultural pursuits, using counseling and involvement in extra-school activities as a means of stimulating school involvement and academic performance among lower-income youngsters. The next step in the demonstration was extensive publicity and the development of popular expectations. The program was expanded to include 100,000 students in 52 elementary and 13 junior high schools at a cost which reached $250 per pupil. As the project was enlarged, it lost its vitality and in 1966 the special apparatus for conducting this demonstration project was abandoned.

The limits of segmental programs of change can also be inferred from the case of the New York City "More Effective Schools Program," which was clearly the most ambitious and comprehensive demonstration program to improve "urban education." In 21 program schools, per pupil costs were raised to almost twice the average instructional costs. It is true that the bulk of the increased costs was allocated for reduced classroom size. The program with its special character and widespread publicity should have developed and probably did result in some Hawthorne effect—producing results merely because of the attention generated by an experiment. Nevertheless, an evaluation study of the "More Effective Schools Program" was most discouraging and symbolized the end of a phase in urban education demonstration that began in the early 1960's with the allocation of private foundation funds.[17] The "More Effective Schools Program" put into practice many segmental innovations that had been recommended, and it was able to carry them out with large-scale funds and resources. In the fall of 1967, the evaluation report was is-

[17] David J. Fox, *Expansion of the More Effective Schools Program; Evaluation of New York City Title I Educational Projects, 1966–1967* (New York: The Center for Urban Education, 1967).

sued after 10 of the schools had been in operation since 1964 and 11 others since 1965. The report, prepared by David J. Fox, concluded that the program had had no significant impact. The overall school climate, staff attitudes, and community relationships had improved, but there was no significant impact on the academic achievement of the pupils. The author assessed that the major weakness of the demonstration effort was the "inexperience and lack of preparation of teachers," factors in part outside the scope of the design of the demonstration. In effect, the evaluation study, as is so often the case with evaluation studies, pointed to larger organizational factors, in this case first, the demand and supply of teachers and second, their preparation and their need for intensive training.

But this project, like most efforts at educational innovation, needs a more penetrating evaluation than it received. The focus of the evaluation was on academic achievement, and on short-term consequences at that, although there also was a concern with staff school climate attitudes and school-community relations. But clearly, the significance of the demonstration program, as in the case of the transformation of mental health institutions, rests primarily in its ability to create a social and moral climate in the school compatible with the values of the larger society. Therefore, as long as academic grades are used as the basic criteria of success, the evaluation studies of slum schools are either naive or self-defeating. Vocational and academic success may well be delayed, but the development of the appropriate social and moral climate should be an end in and of itself. It should be a demonstration that the school system has accepted the responsibility of treating its pupils with fundamental dignity and of enhancing their self-respect. It would imply that the school is fully cognizant of the gap between the family and social background of low-income groups and the behavior desired of the school. But the establishment of the appropriate school setting or milieu is of the highest pragmatic importance if youngsters are to develop in time their vocational and academic skills and interests. In fact, such experiences are not likely to be achieved within the confines of the school but require group recreational, cultural, and work experiences outside of the school in the larger society.

Thus, the evaluation of the "More Effective Schools Program," and a great variety of other such programs, has helped to bring the first phase in "inner city" experimentation to a conclusion. This first phase, roughly designated from 1960 to 1967, emphasized piecemeal change, the demonstration project, and the process of change from the bottom up or by lateral diffusion. It is not to be concluded that no progress was made. There has been a great deal of social learning, but of course, this whole first phase might well have been avoided or more readily terminated by more rational analysis and more forthright leadership. The emerging second phase is that of strategic innovation, or institutional building, which focuses on the system as a whole. It involves a strategy from the top down, it is more comprehensive in scope, and it is concerned with the realities of authority and decision-making. The purpose of this analysis is to explicate sociological concepts that might help in the organizational transformation of public education.

Obviously, more than a conceptual framework is required. Political and professional leadership is central, but the contribution of social scientists remains that of supplying a conceptual framework. The initial step in formulating a change-oriented conceptual framework is to present a characterization of the school system of the inner city as a bureaucratic structure. The school as a social institution has characteristics and features that conform to generalized notions of any large-scale organization; but it also has very distinctive characteristics that arise out of its particular goals and its operational logic.

2. Organizational Format: Image and Reality

The public school system of the inner city, and especially its administrative apparatus, has come under severe and repeated criticism. These censurings have produced a set of popular images about school administration which are based on a sense of frustration rather than on careful analysis of organizational realities. The result is that the urban public school system is viewed by citizen leadership and even experts as an excessively rigid organization that has great difficulty in dealing with innovation, whether the issue be academic content, vocational program, or social climate. The rigidities of the system mean that it has a low capacity to meet the needs of whole groups of students as well as of individual youngsters. At least four images grounded in sophisticated notions of administrative behavior are repeatedly applied to the public school. The public school system of the inner city is viewed as having (a) a highly overcentralized organization, (b) a uniform format, (c) "overprofessionalized" personnel, and (d) a lack of standards of performance. Each of these popular images is oversimplified and needs to be redefined.

CENTRALIZED ORGANIZATION

First, in the image of the alert outsider, the inner city school system is a highly overcentralized organization, which is a core factor in accounting for the lack of innovation and absence of

24

flexibility. Thus the Booz, Allen, and Hamilton management survey of the Chicago system, prepared in 1967 as James Redmond assumed the post of general superintendent, repeated this point of view. "From an organizational viewpoint, the Chicago system is highly centralized. Central office personnel have responsibility for the implementation of these programs in the schools. Relatively few decisions of substance are made in the field. Generally, only routine-action is taken without central office approval." In describing the relationship between the Board of Education and the general superintendent, the report concluded on the basis of recent history that "out of it has emerged an organizational structure where responsibility and authority are concentrated in a relatively small number of people who administer the programs of the school system on a highly centralized basis." (Pp. 1–2.)

The term overcentralization, as used in this sense, is too imprecise to characterize adequately the decision-making in the big city public school system. There is a profound limitation in the term overcentralization if a distinction is not made between decision-making about long-term goals or organization of the school system versus the procedures for administering the organization on a day-to-day basis. It is of course abundantly true that in short-term allocations of resources, in the management of personnel, and in the modification of operating procedures, the approval of a few officials is required and in this respect, decision-making is highly centralized. Nonetheless, centralization of authority at the top levels of the big city school system is reduced and diffused by elements outside the institution. Such authority is greatly reduced by the statutory and legal restraints which narrow the scope of authority of the Board of Education and its superintendent in the strategic management of the organization. Thus, state law has developed a web of rules and regulations which limit the scope of change by defining rigidly many procedures and setting professional standards. The superintendent is even limited in the appointment of his key assistants. The impact of schools of education has removed from the superintendent effective jurisdiction over the training of personnel. Professional associations and commercial groups have strong influence on curriculum and educational procedures.

Moreover, the concept of centralization fails to reflect the diffuse process by which educational-goals policy is established. Although the typical operating school is a relatively self-contained organization (a relatively closed institution in organizational terms), the top management of public school systems is subject to continuous and variegated restraints and pressures that limit its effective authority. The Board of Education typically cannot be viewed as an integrated group which is able to impose its will on the superintendent, but rather as a legislative-type forum in which varying community groups are engaged in a process of balancing conflicting interests. Only in a rare case can the board, through a coalition of political party interests and business groups, develop sufficient cohesion to make a fundamental policy change.

Superintendents often present the image of strong figures and are at times able to dominate their organizational apparatus personally. But the administrative format of the typical large-scale system defies the emergence of a truly centralized system. The lines of authority are generally vague and the central staff lacks the information, resources, and training to make for truly effective centralized decision-making. Compared to industrial corporations, the central staff is truly a "primitive" organization.

Central planning in the educational system is done by *ad hoc* committees. In the absence of effective staff work, these committees are usually manned by line officers who are removed from their operating responsibilities for a few hours or a few days. An atmosphere of constant turmoil and instability, of rushing from one crisis to the next, pervades the system. Centralization is limited fundamentally by the lack of adequate information available at the top levels, due in part to the diffuse criteria of judging educational performance and to the sheer absence of adequate internal information systems.

UNIFORM FORMAT

In the popular image, the inner city school system is seen as a highly uniform and routinized enterprise with little capability for change or flexibility. There can be no doubt that this image reflects the reality of limited effectiveness, but direct observation of the actual working of a big city school system highlights the wide variation in practices and approaches from school to school. Large city school systems are very highly centralized with regard to the formal standards for recruiting and utilizing personnel in the development of an official curriculum, and in many administrative procedures. In day-to-day operations, however, urban schools display weak articulation between the individual school and the central office. Individual principals have considerable operational latitude to make decisions to mobilize resources if they are so inclined. The principal plays a crucial role in what variations do exist and in the higher levels of teaching performance that can be found. The principal affects the recruitment, retention, and morale of the teaching staff, as is well known. He enjoys considerable power and can institute a variety of changes, even if they are only temporary—that is, for the duration of his tenure. It is not unknown for principals to alter radically the grading and tracking system in a manner at variance with customary practice in the system. In particular, the principal can have a considerable role in shaping the social milieu of his school. If he operates successfully, it is because he is a vigorous entrepreneur and is able to mobilize additional resources both within the system and in the community at large.

But this type of "freedom" does not make for long-term development. Each school is a comparatively isolated institution characterized by specific vertical communication patterns. There is a relative absence of lateral communication among principals in the large urban school system. In many cities, because of the pressures of their work load and because of their high mobility from school to school, principals are not as deeply involved in professional or local neighborhood associations as are their counterparts in suburban systems. Instead, urban school principals frequently are oriented toward pursuing higher degrees in graduate schools of education—where the program content seems to bear only a limited relationship to the immediate operating problems facing them in the inner city. The principal operates without adequate professional or organizational support for effective innovation and is much more an isolated specialist compared with the doctor or lawyer, where formal and informal networks supply the effective cohorts of professionalization.

In turn, principals, if they wish—and this is more typically the case—can resist change and innovation. Each school principal operates as a kind of local chieftain. It would be more accurate to describe the inner city school system as fractionalized rather than overcentralized. Perhaps the most striking feature of the United States local school, in contrast to most European systems, is the absence of a system of meaningful on-the-spot inspection which operates both as a means of audit and control and at the same time as a device of assistance and communication to the local principal. The result is a weak and disarticulated system that is subject to continuous crisis and which of necessity must develop a defensive and reactive stance when confronted with new public demands. The operating logic of this fractionalized system is to defend existing practices, rather than to generate clear-cut requirements about the resources required to achieve the tasks assigned to it by its clients and by the larger society.

OVERPROFESSIONALIZATION

The notion of overcentralization and uniformity is paralleled by a popular and vague image of overprofessionalization of teachers. This image is supposed to describe the excessive concern with formal education, formal certification, and professional status. The public school teaching profession has been heavily concerned with formal requirements as a basis for raising professional status and income. This pressure has led to an emphasis on rigid entrance and training requirements often unrelated to actual teaching requirements. Thus, it is true that the teaching profession has resisted the introduction of subprofessionals and other labor intensive approaches to mass education. In this sense, teaching is overprofessionalized.

But the very notion of professionalism is difficult to apply to public school teachers. Some writers concerned with the problems of overprofessionalization have sought to introduce the term "craft" to describe more adequately the skills involved in elementary and secondary school teaching. Moreover, the concept of professionalization is too arbitrary to supply a meaningful basis for understanding the dilemmas and strains that the classroom teacher must face. Rather than speak of overprofessionalization as the pathology of the classroom teacher, it is more accurate to highlight the excessive professional isolation of the classroom teacher in an inner city school, an isolation even greater than that of the school principal.

These concepts should not obscure the realities of classroom teaching in general, and especially classroom teaching in a tough slum school. Teaching youngsters is a profoundly enervating task; under the pressures of the slum school environment, the task has debilitating elements. Adults must gain their gratifications from interaction with other adults, for the responses that youngsters can offer are both consciously and unconsciously incomplete for adult psychic needs. In small communities with stable residential population and in earlier historical periods, the grammar school teacher developed her basic job gratification from the fact that she maintained contact with her pupils as they grew up. She could see them through their letters and return visits as adults, and their behavior and accomplishments as adults were important ingredients in her work satisfaction.[1]

The sheer wear and tear on the teachers and the resulting drain on their energy are powerful pressures. For example, classroom teaching is more of a personal and psychological strain than nursing, but the cohesion and solidarity of the work group in the hospital is much greater than in the public school; in part, nurses serve more as team members. Retreat into indifference and excessive detachment is clearly an understandable response. Thus, teachers require professional and colleague support to meet these pressures. But in its current organization teaching is a solo practice profession, in contrast to many other professions which emphasize group practice or at least close colleague relations. In the typical slum school, teachers do not have close personal and social contacts with their colleagues. Direct supervision and the opportunity for staff conferences is limited. The result is not over-professionalization in the actual performance of the job, but

---

[1] The social history of the teacher, especially the old-fashioned but highly effective spinster teacher, needs to be written. These women were able to develop satisfactory gratification from working with youngsters. But old-fashioned spinsters have passed from the scene because of the new personal freedom which eliminates that particular characterological type.

rather professional isolation and excessive vulnerability to the impact of the social and administrative environment of the slum school.

STANDARDS OF PERFORMANCE

Third, the public school system is viewed by many specialists as an organization that suffers because of an absence of standards of performance; that is, it lacks criteria for judging effectiveness and efficiency. The comparison is frequently made with industrial and business corporations where economic cost and profit supply clear-cut standards. As a result, there is increasing pressure to construct more meaningful standards of performance which would incorporate or at least parallel the procedures of cost effectiveness. Educators are able to offer powerful counter-arguments that the standards of performance in education are diffuse and are of necessity very difficult to operationalize.

There can be no doubt, however, that marked improvement in statistical reporting in public education is required. Moreover, the search for more valid quantitative measures of performance is a challenging intellectual task. But it is a grave error to overlook the existing system of reporting and the existing standards of performance. A great deal of effort is expended in maintaining student attendance records, required in order to document state aid. These records are generally kept on the basis of an outmoded technology, in some cases still by hand and seldom organized to be of relevance to the internal management of the school.

But the basic record-keeping or standards of performance, aside from the regular grading system, is the intelligence and achievement testing system. There are two basic weaknesses in these procedures. First, the tests are not used to assist the individual youngster to diagnose and to improve his performance, and second, the procedures are oriented to evaluating the individual student, rather than also evaluating the teacher, the principal, the school district, or the educational system.

There has been much criticism of the testing procedure as having social and cultural bias and not having high validity.[2] Of course, it can be argued that employers place too high an emphasis on academic performance for many positions and this works against lower-class Negroes; but this is a very different issue. In effect the fairness and validity of the tests is not the central issue, especially at the primary grade levels. If youngsters are to develop reading and academic skills these tests, especially the achievement tests, have relevance as measures of performance and achievement. The basic question is the management and utilization of testing. The danger results when testing becomes a device for thwarting the interests and energies of youngsters from inadequate backgrounds. In slum schools, intelligence and achievement testing are collected at periodic intervals—often at infrequent intervals. The youngsters develop no understanding of the goals or meaning of the testing procedures and are seldom given an opportunity to examine in detail their performance so that they could learn about the sources of their weaknesses. In the slum school, youngsters who are unprepared to perform in terms of national standards enter the school with relatively positive attitudes toward the system. By the end of the third or fourth grade, a great many have failed at least one grade; many have failed twice. The result is that failure becomes the norm, with negative results for both teacher and pupil. The results are not used by the teacher as a basis for developing supplementary work for the particular youngster. They are not used as a means for measuring progress, but rather as an absolute norm or standard. In the end, they become another device of negatively characteriz-

[2] David A. Goslin, *The Search for Ability* (New York: John Wiley & Sons, 1966).

ing the student in the slum school. Nevertheless, there is sufficient experience to indicate that sensitive teachers and volunteer workers in community education projects have used tests successfully as diagnostic devices and as a criterion for ascertaining progress.

At the high school level the testing system can have negative impact for inner city school students, since it serves to lower the aspirations of the students who perform inadequately. But the system is even more rigid and distorted since research indicates that in high school the same level of performance leads to different grades, depending on the social background of students; students from families of lower background, with similar measured potential, receive lower grades than do students from families of higher social background.[3] The ranking system is part of a system of social control that maintains social inequality. The grades are a reward system and their distribution becomes a technique for managing and controlling the student body. Dropouts are not limited to inferior students. Once students with adequate IQ scores at the high school level recognize that they are not likely to be adequately rewarded, they withdraw; to do otherwise would almost be irrational.

Second, much of the grading and the testing system, because it is oriented to reporting on the student rather than on the teacher or the school, is not easily used as a management tool. The essential task is to convert the testing and record-keeping procedures into a system for evaluating teacher and organizational effectiveness. The question becomes not the particular student's grades, but, for example, the relative capacity of a school to cut down dropout rates, or to produce progress in academic achievement

[3] Rosemary G. Sarri and Robert D. Vinter, "Group Work for the Control of Behavioral Problems in Secondary Schools," in David Street (ed.), *Innovation in Mass Education* (New York: John Wiley & Sons, 1969).

levels. The record-keeping system and criteria of performance need to be developed as devices for insuring the rights of individual pupils, that is, for guaranteeing a system of due process. It is depressing to observe the extent to which students in a slum school can be denied services simply because of inadequate records. Moreover, the issue runs deeper. Because the public school system is a relatively closed system without appropriate grievance procedures, parents must individually negotiate on behalf of their youngsters, if they have the skill and motivation, and often in a most indirect fashion. In the case of a slum school, parents either have withdrawn or are excluded. More effective records about the performance of teachers and schools would supply a new basis for auditing and evaluating public education.

Thus, the image of the school system of the inner city as an organization which operates on the basis of (a) overcentralization, (b) organizational uniformity, and (c) the absence of criteria or performance, gives way to a more differentiated view of its organizational format. This view is a starting point for a conceptual model of change.

3. Alternative Models of Change

One underlying assumption of this analysis of the inner city school system is that a crucial barrier to strategic change and increased effectiveness of public school systems is the absence of comprehensive conceptual models.[1] To speak of the importance of conceptual models of education is obviously not an academic exercise that is oblivious to the political and social elements required to produce actual change. Institution building in public education cannot be accomplished by any single drastic or dramatic act. Schools cannot be transformed by boycotts or parents' strikes, although these demonstrations may speed up the process of reform. School systems are too complex to respond to the mere appointment of a new superintendent. Likewise changes in the system of recruiting board members or plans for decentralization may be essential for organizational development, but are only preconditions.

In the American scene, there have been powerful constraints against a positive and direct involvement by elected municipal officials in the management of the school system. In the past, explosive religious differences have threatened public education when the management of the school system became directly in-

[1] This is but an alternative specification of the idea that increased financial resources alone will not produce the type of school that is able to meet the demands of society.

volved in partisan politics. The highly pluralistic nature of American politics has meant that elected political leadership exercised narrow influence on educational institutions, and only indirectly.

During the last decade, however, elected officials have cautiously expanded their involvement in educational policy. The sheer increase in local, state, and Federal expenditures has required their more active participation. Elected officials have had to confront questions of the adequacy of the contemporary mechanisms of local, state, and national governments for administering fiscal aid to education. They have had to search for standards of need and meaningful standards of performance. In fact, isolated elected officials have questioned fundamental notions about which aspects of mass education belong in the public or private sector or what new combinations are required. Conceptual models are designed in part to supply political leaders and educational professionals with a more common language of discourse.[2]

THE MENTAL HEALTH MODEL

Because of professional concern with the slum school, it was inevitable that there would be efforts to impose the strategy of the mental health movement directly on the school system, to develop an organizational model that fundamentally parallels the therapeutic setting. These specialists have been advocating that

[2] If there has been an absence of holistic models to assist innovation and change, there is no shortage of broad-scale attacks on the public schools as social institutions. From the radical left and from conservative sources, writers of considerable force have offered both searching criticisms and educational utopias. These writings carry considerable weight in the public debate about American education.

For the radical left, see Paul Goodman, *Growing Up Absurd* (New York: Random House, Inc., 1960); for the conservative approach to the reaffirmation of fundamentals, see Hyman Rickover, *Education and Freedom* (New York: E. P. Dutton & Co., Inc., 1959).

the slum school became less of a "custodial" institution and be more positive in its "treatment" impact. Numerous reservations can be formulated about such an approach but these efforts are noteworthy because of their comprehensive intentions.

This approach assumes that the resources of the family in the slum are so limited or its values so at variance with the goals of the school that the school must seek to become responsible for the total social space of the child. The model falls just short of formulating a residential institution, but every effort is made to come as close as possible to a residential approach. (In Great Britain, there has been discussion of government-financed boarding schools, which would make available to working-class children the same advantages offered a middle-class child at boarding school.)

The teacher becomes the teacher-counselor in a manner not dissimilar to the residential treatment center, as, for example, Bruno Bettelheim's Orthogenic School.[3] This approach calls for a drastic reduction in teacher-pupil ratios to about one to fifteen or even one to ten. If possible the teacher-counselor should remain with her class as long as possible in order to develop stable interpersonal relations. Within existing public systems there are individual principals who seek to implement such an approach of the school as a "home away from home."[4] The teacher-counselor rejects, or at least reduces, reliance on a complex division of labor and personally intervenes to help insure that the needs and services required by each child are made available. The housing, feeding, and clothing of each child is a school responsibility that must

[3] Bruno Bettelheim and E. Sylvester, "Milieu Therapy—Indications and Illustrations," *Psychoanalytical Review*, 36 (1) (1949), 54–68.

[4] Elements for such an approach are described in the profile, "The Principal," *The New Yorker* (May 7, 1966), 55 ff., which deals with the work of Elliot Shapiro at P.S. 119, New York City; reprinted in Nat Hentoff, *Our Children Are Dying* (New York: The Viking Press, Inc., 1966).

come under the surveillance of the teacher and the principal. Likewise, the teacher sets the pace and guides the formal educational program, but only in the light of the interpersonal need and social reality of the child. The teacher is truly the substitute for the parents, with the clear recognition that the parents have been and continue to be unable to meet the needs of the child. It is not by accident that those involved in such programs have had experience as staff members in mental hospitals or treatment institutions.

Criticism of such a model derives not from its costly character. The costs of such an approach may well be the basic costs that society has to pay. There is little adequate knowledge about the societal costs of alternative programs, or the current costs of not having effective educational programs. Reservations and limitations derive from two other sets of considerations. First is the theoretical issue of the impact on the socialization of youngsters that would result from such an educational model: What types of interpersonal strengths and dependencies are likely to be generated? The teacher-counselor model is a modification of the classic two-person psychotherapy, but it is an approach that is still grounded in notions of transference or at least the necessity for strong interpersonal identifications as a basis for changing personal motives and gratifications. The teacher-counselor model seeks to manage the total educational environment in order to facilitate the restructuring of motives and to broaden the opportunity for interacting with adults and peers who can serve as stimulants for positive response. The basic thrust is to establish stable and gratifying interpersonal relations. In effect, there is a built-in proclivity toward seeking to extend and enlarge the relations between the teacher-counselor and her particular group of youngsters. Such stable and gratifying relations are seen as prerequisites to educational involvement and advocates hold that such attachments are essential for the process of maturation. Critics, however, feel that the impact of such intense relations with teachers would produce an adjustment to the school and not to the large society. It would be equivalent to the "prisonization" syndrome, where the model prisoner performs well under custody but fails when he is returned to the outer world.

These critics point out that, given the mobility and disruption of social life in the slum, there is a strong element of unreality in these efforts. Only a small portion of youngsters are likely to develop relatively enduring relations with a teacher-counselor. The counter-argument is that a teacher-counselor may introduce an element of stability into the lives of these youngsters. For example, there is case material to demonstrate that effective teachers can help youngsters persuade their families to give up the practice of repeated and pointless residential mobility, nurtured by frustration and boredom.

Second, and more pointed, critics are concerned with the problem of translating the model into an organization system. The problems of staffing such an educational enterprise seem immense, but the basic dilemma is deeper than the sheer supply of appropriate personnel, difficult though that may be. How would such a system operate and maintain its effectiveness? An organization cannot function on the basis of the sheer energy of its constituent elements, but requires a division of labor and a system of effective supports. Any conventional administrative apparatus would by its very nature tend to thwart many positive elements of this approach.

But one has only to observe directly the social climate of a classroom or a school where these notions are operative to recognize that any system of improved academic effectiveness must rest on the creation of a classroom climate based on mutual respect or value sharing, to use Harold Lasswell's terminology. A school based on these conceptions can operate as a public yard-stick and serve as criteria to be taken into consideration by edu-cational administrators. Even if the teacher-counselor model is not generalizable, it is an important element in a comprehensive effort at institution building.

THE EARLY EDUCATION MODEL

The difficulty of applying the teacher-counselor system or other equivalent notions on a comprehensive basis has led to efforts to formulate partial strategies based on dynamic psychology. The early education movement is clearly the most massive expres-sion of an effort at a compromise. If the school cannot become a residential institution then at least the school can intervene ear-lier and thus be more effective. This has special relevance for the youngster of the slum family where parental impact has been demonstrated to inhibit and retard intellectual and cognitive processes. Early education has had the administrative advantage that progress could be made without having to deal with the fun-damental problems of existing school organization, as most of these programs were established outside of existing structures or with their minimal cooperation. Again, one has only to observe the vitality of many of the preschool education programs that have been initiated by Federal funds to appreciate their validity and to anticipate that such experiences will gradually become part of the educational experience of youngsters.

Over the short run, however, early education efforts were very costly to develop. They failed to have maximum impact because children who had such experiences subsequently entered conven-tionally organized school systems. Perhaps one of the most power-ful direct results of these efforts was to stimulate the interest of parents in the education of their youngsters, and to develop stronger political interests and even political activity related to education, including demands for black cultural separation.

At best the early education movement can be considered another partial strategy. At worst, it was a basic error in priorities. A partial strategy of change which allocated highest priority to the preschool youngster is a reflection of a concern for the management of the individual rather than with the management of the slum community. The counter-strategy of intervention with the oldest school-age groups seems more plausible. In a slum community, the fourteen- to eighteen-year-old males have the greatest impact on the moral and social climate of the school. In this group are opinion leaders in the slum youth culture and the effective bearers of the culture of the slum from one generation to the next. If these youngsters develop a sense of frustration and a group life in opposition to the goals of the school, as they generally do, they are able to frustrate innovation. The case can be made that this group represents the highest priority, not the youngest group, if comprehensive change is to be effected.

SPECIALIZATION AND AGGREGATION MODELS

In contrast to the mental health and early education approaches, the strategy of this analysis is to present two alternative models of organizational change in educational institutions: the *specialization model* and the *aggregation model*. Both of these models see the school as a social institution. These models supply criteria for judging and evaluating specific research findings and particular innovations. They are offered as a basis for describing many current practices and for assessing efforts at strategic innovation. It is not enough to point out that they are both hypothetical constructs. The specialization model is in effect an expression of the major trends over the last decade of innovation programs. It encompasses a variety of the current segmental and administrative changes. There are very few examples of meaningful or persistent innovation that conform to the aggregation model but they do exist. It is much more than an ideal model; it is a notion of potentialities. The aggregation model is the expression of administrators and staff members who are concerned primarily with a basic format within which change and effective teaching can take place. Specific programs and specific techniques are of secondary concern, as compared with organizational climate, institutional milieu, or operational doctrine. My preference is clearly for the aggregation model, and this needs to be explicitly acknowledged. In Chart 1 the basic dimensions of both models are presented.

Both the specialization model and the aggregation model focus on the classroom teacher. The capacity of the public school system to achieve its goals, both academic and social, involves a central concern with increasing the authority and professional competence of the teacher. The dilemmas that the teaching profession face are characteristic of every other professional group, resulting from increased available knowledge, the increased complexity of the professional tasks that need to be performed, and societal demands for higher levels of performance.

Fundamentally, the specialization model appears to be an *ad hoc* adaptation by introducing, on a piecemeal basis, new techniques, new programs, new specialists, and even new specific administrative procedures, each of which may appear valid. On the other hand, the aggregation model focuses on the totality of the situation in which the teacher finds herself.[5]

Under the specialization model, the traditional activity of the teacher is modified as the teaching process is broken up into more and more specialized roles. The increased level of substantive knowledge and the importance of specific teaching techniques are offered as the rationale for the teachers' subordination to curricu-

[5] See David A. Goslin, "The School in a Changing Society: Notes on the Development of Strategies for Solving Educational Problems," *American Journal of Orthopsychiatry* Vol. XXXVII, No. 5 (October, 1967), p. 843.

lum specialists. The complexities of deviant behavior are given as the reason for their subordination to experts in the management of interpersonal relations. In contrast, the aggregation model emphasizes the necessity for maintaining and strengthening the teacher's role as the central manager of the classroom in which he creates the conditions for teaching and learning. In this model, teaching is seen as a diffuse relationship to the pupil and leadership skills are as important as technical proficiency in the subject. The teacher makes use of specialists and resource personnel, but manages their introduction into the classroom. The term "aggregation" is designed to draw attention to the adding up of the parts of the social system in which the teacher must operate. The aggregation model recognizes that teacher-pupil relations involve direct and immediate response. This model is deeply influenced with the notion of teacher-counselor but it is not the same. The teacher-counselor is a single person who personally seeks, as much as possible, to serve the needs of a classroom of youngsters.

The aggregation model also places the teacher, or more accurately the teacher-administrator, in charge of a group of youngsters. He is responsible for the well-being and educational progress of these youngsters. But the teacher can involve a variety of persons, both within and outside the school, to see that the youngster has access to the basic needs and values. In fact, the aggregation model fundamentally is concerned with expanding the pool of such human resources for the individual youngster. There is no way of knowing in advance to whom a student will relate appropriately and who will in effect offer satisfactory and stable interpersonal contacts. It is the function of the teacher-manager to see that such relationships are facilitated.

The specialization and aggregation models rest on differing assumptions about human nature and the strategy of learning. The specialization model is actively buttressed by an elaborate in-

CHART 1

BASIC DIMENSIONS OF SPECIALIZATION AND AGGREGATION MODEL

Dimension	Specialization Model	Aggregation Model
Strategy of Change	Incremental innovation by specific programs. Piecemeal change based on demonstration programs.	Holistic reorganization reflecting concern with organizational climate and minimum standards. Based on top level managerial direction.
Organization Goals	Priority of academic over socialization; socialization stressed but segregated.	Interdependence of academic and socialization goals.
Division of Labor	Emphasis on increased division of labor and increased use of specialists.	Emphasis on increased authority and professional competence of classroom teacher.
Investment Pattern	Capital intensive techniques; high investment on the new media.	Labor intensive techniques; stress on subprofessionals and volunteers.
Organizational Format	School district central office levels with central office exercising administrative control.	Schools under sectors' administrative control, with central office planning control.
Authority Structure	Fractionalized.	Centralized policy-making and decentralization based on professional autonomy.
Curriculum Construction	External and centralized construction; independent hierarchy of curriculum specialists in school system.	Balance between external construction of materials and faculty involvement in curriculum construction; curriculum specialists as resource personnel.
Grading System	Fixed class levels, periodic grading on systemwide criteria.	Continuous development system, flexible system of grading which include both systemwide criteria and specific indicators of achievement.
School Districts	Specific and single boundaries with trend toward specialized schools.	Multiple and flexible boundaries and emphasis on adaptation of comprehensive high school.

CHART 1—*Continued*

Dimension	Specialization Model	Aggregation Model
Principal's Role	Administrative specialist.	Principal teacher.
Teacher's Role	(a) Teacher specialist; specialized skills and subject matter oriented;	(a) Teacher manager balance between subject matter skills and interpersonal and managerial competence;
	(b) Academic and vocational training.	(b) Coordinator of social space of youngster and of community resources.
Classroom Management	Reduction of class size.	Flexible educational groupings depend on program.
Teaching Style	Solo practitioner.	Group practice; peer group support and use of subprofessionals and volunteers.
Subprofessionals and Volunteers	Limited involvement and narrow definition of tasks.	Strong emphasis; seen as general resource with teaching responsibilities.
Psychology of Learning	Cognitive psychology.	Impact of institutional setting and normative order.
Control of Deviant Behavior	Emphasis on specialized personnel and specialized structure.	Maximize classroom management and teacher skills.
Evaluation	Pupil oriented.	Teacher and system oriented.
New Media	Centralized control, used for regular instruction, for maximum audience manned by media personnel.	Decentralized control use for specific audiences as a supplement to regularized instruction.
Community Contacts	Specific, directed through principal and specialized community agent.	Diffuse and involvement of all educational staff members.
Teacher Education	Specialized education in education and classroom practice teaching.	Liberal arts education plus clinic exposure to diversified experiences in community and educational practice.
Inservice Training	Under the control of school of education and linked to degrees.	Under public school system control and linked to professional development and curriculum development.

tellectualized psychology of learning which is rooted in individual and cognitive psychology. The specialization model has as its goal the elaboration of cognitive processes and the enhancement of academic achievement mainly brought about by reconstructing the contents of the curriculum according to the principles of cognitive development.

Educational psychologists supply a partial rationale for the specialization model, although they would criticize many of the actual applications of their principles into practice. Basically, these educational psychologists have sought to broaden the definition of the maximum amount of the student's ability to learn. Led by the recommendations of Jerome S. Bruner, the dominant intellectual posture of educational psychologists had been to question traditional conceptions of readiness for learning.[6] Their conclusion is that educators have vastly underemphasized the capacities of children to learn. The key to the learning process, from this point of view, is to restructure the subject matter—the curriculum content—so that it articulates with fundamental principles of intellectual and cognitive development of the child. The consequence of this perspective—even though it may be an unanticipated consequence—is to create a group of specialists whose impact is felt through a restructuring of the curriculum, without adequate regard for the full institutional milieu. In this sense it is part of the specialization model.

But the existence of a body of general principles, grounded in research, is still a problematic issue. Therefore, the central notion of the new curriculum development movement is stated in the following terms by Bruner: "We begin with the hypothesis that any subject can be taught effectively in some intellectually honest

[6] Jerome S. Bruner, *The Process of Education* (New York: Vintage Books, 1960).

form to any child at any state of development."[7] Such an assertion is patently not a hypothesis but a moral exhortation since it rests on the crucial and completely ambiguous term "honest."

Suppose it were the case that the process of the child's intellectual development offered by Jean Piaget and adapted by Bruner supported the claim that any subject can effectively be taught at any stage of human development. But then the issue would still exist as to what should be taught at what age to serve the individual's and society's needs. Piaget himself has questioned the American adaptation and application of his thinking to curriculum reform.[8] He emphasizes developmental stages to a much greater extent than Bruner would and questions the American emphasis on speeding up the learning process. Moreover, a gap between Piaget's concept and the realities of classroom teaching must exist, for Piaget never thought of his work as the basis of specific instructions to teachers. His work and the efforts that it has stimulated have meaning for the classroom teacher not because they supply engineering-type guides for curriculum development, but because, directly or indirectly, they increase the interpersonal capacity of the classroom teacher. In the specialization model, the psychologist makes his impact felt through his general principles of learning, which in turn influence the specialist on curriculum construction teams. In the aggregation model, the psychologist has the same relation to the teacher as the teacher has to her pupil —a direct and diffuse one in which there is a continuous process of interaction.

The end result of the curriculum development movement, based on the theory of cognition, has been an additional pressure

[7] *Ibid.,* 33.
[8] Frank G. Jennings, "Jean Piaget: Notes on Learning," *Saturday Review,* 50 (May 20, 1967), 81–83.

toward educational rigidity with a commitment to a spiral curriculum and its mechanical emphasis on earlier and earlier exposure to more intellectually complicated materials.[9] Its grossest form is present in a quotation from David Page, who has been characterized as one of the most experienced teachers of elementary mathematics: "In teaching from kindergarten to graduate school, I have been amazed at the intellectual similarity of human beings at all ages, although children are perhaps more spontaneous, creative and more energetic than adults."[10]

Instead of such a perspective, under the aggregation model the principles of curriculum construction depend not only on cognitive (rational) processes but, equally, on affective (emotional) considerations. Thus, for example, there is a considerable body of experience which indicates that the limitation in reading achievement among these youngsters is based on the fact that they are weaker in comprehension than they are in vocabulary or speed. The experiences of skilled teachers and volunteers lead to the hypothesis that breaking up the curriculum into component parts according to some principles of developmental learning and repeated instruction does not necessarily serve these youngsters. To the contrary, these youngsters require a more configurational approach in which the interrelations of component elements are stressed and the students presented with an opportunity to respond to the elements in a variety of settings.

Concern with the structuring of materials is of less importance than the sheer question of mobilizing interest in the subject matter. A central question is a set of rewards and pattern of motivation which lead youngsters to undertake the necessary "intellec-

---

[9] In fact, curriculum reform has many elements of a social movement with strong overtones of romantic ideology in which the children have the role of saviors of mankind by their classroom exploits.

[10] Bruner, *op. cit.*, 39.

tual" struggle and effort. These rewards are most effective if they are immediate, mediated through personal relations, and are strengthened if they are unconditional. Frustration and instability of interpersonal relations are all at work. Academic exploration outside of one's immediate life space can become difficult and even at times painful. Human beings and human referents are the most effective carriers of meaning, not abstractions. The case of a twelve-year-old girl who could not comprehend the notion of the United States or "our country" is illustrative. Efforts to develop an understanding of these words failed when maps and charts were used. The tutor succeeded when, by accident, she presented the girl with a picture of President Kennedy standing next to an American flag. The girl was able to identify the flag as the "Kennedy flag," and from that it was possible to introduce the notion of her own flag and in turn to develop an association to our own country and the concept of the United States.

In short, compensatory education must confront elements of a powerful egocentrism. The teachers and the materials they use need to be able to convince the youngster that they are concerned with his basic needs. It is no accident that the after-school study centers, as part of their procedures, feed youngsters, and there is no effort to withhold food as part of the incentive system. In developing the details of the aggregation model, strong emphasis is placed on making available to the youngster tutorial assistance offered by one person. The youngster who is falling behind wants to command the attention of a single person; even assistance in a small group, valuable as it may be, hardly suffices to reach the core of his internal pressures. This in turn leads to those recommendations that stress intensive human effort rather than elaborate but impersonal technology.

The effective teacher is one who is able to personalize the curriculum and present it as projecting her own personality and presence. The effective teacher, on the basis of her own efforts, must be able to implement this notion regardless of the official content of the curriculum. This involves a fundamental professional perspective, not a set of specific techniques, although it can be manifested by means as diverse as calling the child by his proper name and not a nickname, the preparation of materials about the youngsters in the classroom, and the creative use of ethnic and racial pride and heritage.

The reservation implied in the aggregation model about a cognitive theory of curriculum reform can be stated in alternative terms. Cognitive psychology is an insufficient basis for institutional building, relevant though it may be. Basically, the theory fails to take into consideration the social class and cultural elements that condition learning and supply the context in which the school as an institution must operate. This is implied in the notion of organizational climate. Thus, by contrast, the aggregation model is grounded in a set of assumptions about the slum school as a normative or moral order in which there are group solidarities and the need for legitimate authority.

The moral order of the slum school cannot be characterized by simple generalizations if only because of the variation from school to school and from classroom to classroom. But more fundamentally there is no necessity to assume that the moral order of any low-income school is by its very nature incompatible with the requirements of a civil society. There are older and relatively stable low-income communities where the school functions on the basis of mutual consent and a relative sense of legitimacy even though its educational effectiveness may be limited, or serve to limit the aspirations of the youngsters it serves.[11] But the slum school in most Negro ghettos has lost much of its legitimacy.

[11] See Gerald Suttles, *The Social Order of the Slum* (Chicago: University of Chicago Press, 1968).

As indicated earlier, the aggregation model makes the assumption that the pupil orientation in the slum school is a mixture of indifference and hostility toward the school authorities. These tensions create a group of student leaders who maintain their position by exploitation and even coercion, since they personify opposition to the school authorities. School authorities seldom if ever seek to cooperate with the most hostile and coercive student leaders as techniques of organizational control. The old-fashioned bully-boy system of the correctional institution in which toughs are used to keep order is generally not to be found in public slum schools. But the presence of these informal leaders blocks efforts of educational reform. School authorities seek to resist such leaders or to export them out of their jurisdiction. Thus, in the typical slum school, the details of curriculum reform based on theories of cognitive development are of secondary importance.

It must be added quickly that the remarkable aspect of the slum high school is that student moral order is differentiated. If there is a minority of outright opposition to educational goals and a majority of indifference, there is also a minority of career-oriented students. Within the confines of the slum school there is a group who "make it," who resist the informal social structure and develop a commitment to academic or vocational involvement. The sources of such commitment are only dimly understood since sociologists have not carried out naturalistic studies of the slum school. This minority subculture is supported, but only inadequately, by the school officials. Those youngsters who succeed are expressing either the consequences of parental support, the influence of a gifted group of teachers, or experience generated in some community agency which helps to stabilize friendship patterns. They may also be expressing sheer personal energy mobilized in opposition to the dominant values surrounding them. The aggregation model seeks a set of educational practices that would transform the normative and moral order of the slum school. At a minimum, school administrators need to neutralize the power position of opposition student leaders and to this end some degree of cooperation with them is not ruled out. The essential issue, however, is that the minority culture of commitment to the school's goals (including its recreational sports and vocational programs) must become a more dominant element in the school milieu. The fundamental value and norm is not future achievement and future occupational goals, but a social system that seeks to strengthen individual dignity and self-respect in the immediate setting. In the simplest terms, whatever else is required, the youngsters must be treated so as to enhance their self-respect.

At any given moment a heavy concentration of youngsters in slum communities as they reach the ages of twelve to fourteen can be described as "alienated." But the concept alienation seems much too global and much too diffuse to be penetrating and revealing. In particular, it fails to highlight the personal and social processes by which these youngsters come to reject the authority and the legitimacy of the school system.

It is difficult to characterize with precision the state of mind and group goals of such youngsters. It is particularly difficult to penetrate their thoughts about their teachers and their principals. One important element is the impact of the mass media on these young people which gives them a rhetoric and vocabulary but which hides their real feelings and emotions.

Even in the absence of extensive and systematic studies in depth, however, a group of themes emerge with sufficient clarity and repetition. These themes are identified not as the result of eavesdropping or violation of personal privacy. Nor is it necessary to erect the barrier that the thoughts of these youngsters are accessible only to other members of their minority or cultural group. Children's direct and explicit expressions of underlying sentiments become exposed when they participate in a rewarding educational and interpersonal experience. This can be seen in the contacts and communications generated in "experimental" programs such as in tutoring groups, in after-school study centers, recreational or work programs that are able to cater to demands for self-respect.

For the bulk of these so-called alienated students, the experience of school—despite its frustrating elements—is their most powerful social experience. No other institution has the same impact, including the church, local recreational agencies, and even the police. Although these students hardly comprehend the logic of school, it is the focal point—positive and negative—of their daily social experience. School is a common experience that offers coordinates in their lives much more so than a family life that is highly unstable and explosive. The school introduces at least an element of uniformity and expectation in their lives.

The educational figures of the school are powerful persons; in fact, for the students, they are all too powerful guardians of their lives. Once the children find themselves in a rewarding and supportive setting, they are prepared to talk endlessly about their teachers. The children seek fair play from their teachers. In root terms, the definition of fair play is the simple ability to keep order, and to accord a relative amount of equality of treatment. The teacher is seen as having a kind of magical power, for frequently the youngsters have little understanding of the relations between her performance and their success or failure in the classroom. As the youngsters proceed through the primary grades, the teachers' aspirations are not unrealistic; rather the youngsters just do not comprehend or master the necessary responses. As a result, the process of hostility and mutual distrust that ultimately develops is speeded up.

Therefore, the distinction between the specialization and the aggregation models also involves different commitments to the appropriate balance of academic or vocational versus socialization goals. Educators have, of course, been traditionally aware that they both transmit skills and inculcate social values. But, in the past, they sought to deal with the issues of priorities and balance mainly in an implicit fashion and as a by-product of their primary commitment to academic and vocational tasks.

In contemporary society, there is considerable concern that the school system prepare youngsters for the "competition" they are to encounter in the "real" world, and therefore, the aggregation model must anticipate a curious argument. This argument runs as follows: If the suburban school system continues as currently organized and the inner city school succeeds in moving toward the aggregation model with its emphasis on self-respect, and on an educational strategy that emphasizes continuous as opposed to age-graded education, would not "the result be a further separation of inner city youngsters and suburban ones in terms of life chances after grammar school." This is a point of view that sees competition—rather than group solidarity—as the basis of educational motivation.

First, this point of view fails to recognize that emphasis on socialization and self-respect is not at the immediate or long-term expense of academic achievement, wherever and whenever it can be effectively achieved. At the risk of repetition the assumption of the aggregation model is that present arrangements do not operate effectively and more intensive and extensive exposure to existing programs will not and have not produced higher levels of academic achievement. Second, and more pointedly, the aggregation model does not rule out or overlook the role of competition in the school or in the "real" world although it recognizes the limits of competition. The aggregation model emphasizes that the inner city youngster first compete with himself and second with his immediate peers, before he is thrown into competition with all of his age group. It holds that merely to emphasize competition is to perpetuate an unequal race that is certain to maintain current privileges and inequalities. Finally, on this point, it needs to be stated that the aggregation model is designed to increase equality of education and to improve individual and group mobility. But equality of educational opportunity and improved education do not alone and directly solve the issues of social change in our society. It is dangerous to have a person's position in society determined exclusively by his performance in school, and it is equally dangerous when school performance guarantees great and persistent degrees of social inequality. In a democratic society, persons must be able to achieve their goals to some measure on the basis of a display of their skills which can continue to grow throughout adult life.

The new "crisis" in public education has meant that educational administrators, especially those in the inner city, must develop a new hierarchy of educational goals. The superintendents of the major big city school systems and their top assistants have been forced to accept the position that academic and vocational achievement is not possible unless the school becomes more directly and explicitly involved in the socialization of its youngsters. This has meant a reformulation of the logic with which they have operated during the formative years of their own administrative careers. Many view the shifting and broadening of goals with considerable skepticism.

The most common response to the expansion of educational perspectives is contained in the repeatedly encountered phrase, "the school cannot do the whole job." From this point of view, which is the dominant view of school administrators, socialization goals are adjunctive or secondary objectives that the school must undertake in order to fill its primary function—the transmission

of skill. Special personnel, special functions, and special programs are added to achieve these adjunct goals. Such a broadening of goals of the public school system, especially in the inner
city, conforms to the specialization model. The specialization
model is an expression of an incremental philosophy of change in
which delimited and specific steps are taken, although it may be
questioned whether the particular steps are powerful enough to
produce the desired objectives.

By contrast, the aggregation model, in theory, emphasizes not
an incremental conception of organizational change, but rather a
concern with minimum standards of performance. Thus, the aggregation model is influenced by the holistic strategy of change of
the mental health movement. What type of organizational structure and what amount of resources are required in order to create
an educational environment and a moral order that would meet
the minimum requirement of effectiveness? With the establishment of basic requirements, step by step, programs become justified. In short, academic or vocational goals are fused with those of
socialization. This is not to say that socialization goals are made
equal to those of academic achievement. They are seen as interdependent. Interdependent means a flexible balance including
the circumstances in which socialization goals, for a particular
time period and for a particular group of students, might well out-
weigh academic or vocational objectives.

The aggregation model does not assert that the addition of specialists in either curriculum development or in the management
of interpersonal relations will insure an adequate social climate
in the public school system. To achieve this goal, the aggregation
model is not limited to an increased emphasis on socialization
processes. To the contrary, the school is seen as the central coordinating mechanism in the personal and social development of the
youngster. The school not only seeks to organize itself to a system

based on mutual self-esteem and dignity; it is also concerned with the entire existence of the youngster outside of the school.

To state that the school becomes the coordinating institution in the lives of its youngsters does not imply that it manages their total life space. It does not mean that the school directs the local health agency, the social agency, or the police in the immediate environment. It means that the requirements of the school serve as the stimulus for insuring relevant policy and practices by all these agencies. In particular, the school and the teacher become the central locus for all information about its students. The school is the only institution, except perhaps for the police, which touches the lives of all the residents. Therefore, this conception means that the school is the point at which the various directed efforts at social change, both public and private, can be meaningfully related.

The school is the essential institution, but the aggregation model does not imply that it becomes the controlling institution in the slum. If the school sought to be a substitute for the family or welfare institutions, it would be destined to fail. But the school, because of its unique characteristics, can operate as a coordinating mechanism for formal and informal programs of intervention. Moreover, this approach is predicated on the notion that a minority of youngsters will not succeed in school. For them the experience of work, military or other forms of vocational service will supply for them, as for earlier generations, essential socialization experience. It is hoped that this minority can be minimized. It is outside the scope of this analysis to deal with the artificial barriers and institutional defects that such youngsters must face.

An additional dimension for exploring the operational elements of the specialization and the aggregation models is derived from reference to the economic distinction between capital versus labor intensive approaches. The specialization model stresses capital intensive measures while the aggregation model stresses that of labor intensive ones. Of course, both approaches are present in each model and the basic issue is the most appropriate combination. Capital intensive methods imply high investment costs which can be used for the training and professionalization of personnel, and the extensive use of complex technological devices. Effectiveness and efficiency result from the high output which each costly input of effort is designed to produce. Labor intensive methods center on the notion that in the educational process there is need for significant amounts of inexpensive effort and simple human resources. This is dictated by the diffuse nature of the teaching function and by the increased emphasis on the fusion of academic and socialization goals. Socialization goals cannot be achieved on a mass basis by capital intensive techniques alone.

It should be noted that the aggregation model asserts that although it emphasizes the incorporation of labor intensive techniques, the coordination and utilization of these resources requires very high levels of managerial expertise. The teacher and principal who can make effective use of volunteers, teacher aides, homework helpers, and adjunct specialists must have additional training, higher levels of professionalization, and higher rewards. In fact, this is the element of professionalization that the aggregation model stresses; the restructuring of work so that teachers can become master teachers and principals become principal-teachers. The capital intensive elements in the aggregation model are therefore to be found in the higher level of professionalization required to utilize effective labor intensive resources.

Thus, in partial summary, the distinction between the specialization and the aggregation models can be highlighted by different emphasis placed on the academic goals versus those of socialization, by the importance given to the school as a coordinating unit of community development, and by the relative stress on capital versus labor intensive approaches.

Finally, both of these models are concerned with the rank-and-file teacher. It is clearly recognized that an outstanding school principal or a gifted classroom teacher can perform with distinction regardless of the administrative system. In fact, there is hardly a school that does not point with pride to its "star" teachers who appropriate for themselves the professional space required for some degree of autonomy and creativity. Frequently, such teachers display very strong personal motivation which leads them to deviate from the immediate organizational climate in which they find themselves. They are often older women who are invulnerable to institutional pressure because of their informal seniority or their commanding personal presence. Likewise, in the large metropolitan school systems, there are individual school principals who disregard the formal and informal system to produce noteworthy but temporary levels of performance. These principals often have strong professional aspirations and feel that they are secure because they can get appointments in smaller systems. Their ranks include an occasional district superintendent with real personal charisma who has given up aspiration for a staff promotion "downtown." But the objective of these two institutional models of change is to increase the effectiveness of the "typical" teacher and the "typical" principal.

The effectiveness of the "typical" teacher is an expression of deliberate managerial efforts of school executives. The administrator has the responsibility to allow the gifted teacher adequate conditions to demonstrate special talents. But an administrator's central concern is to enhance the capacity of the "typical" teacher and this depends on the overall organization of the school system.

Each strategy change implies a different set of operational procedures. The next section sets forth illustrative examples of how these different models of change can and do guide administrative practice. By examining a series of more specific operational tasks, their full implication can be assessed. Among the illustrative problems that warrant examination are classroom management; the use of the new media; teacher education and career lines; authority and decentralization; pupil composition and decentralization; school-community relations.

4. Operational Elements

CLASSROOM MANAGEMENT

The major concern of the specialization model in the management of the classroom is the reduction of class size. This is seen as the crucial variable of change. The national trend toward the reduction of the classroom size has been pushed without abeyance since the turn of the century when the immigrant working-class families sent their children to schools with seventy to ninety pupils per class and educators tried to reduce classes to sixty.[1] The quality of American education has been operationalized in terms of per capita expenditures and that in turn is but a measure of the ratio of teacher to pupils. Since the certified teacher is the most costly item, the major strategy has been a capital intensive one.

The pressure continues to reduce class size in the inner cities. The impact of the psychotherapeutic model and the notion of the teacher-counselor serve to reenforce this trend. In addition, the trade union movement among teachers has made teaching loads a crucial objective rather than emphasizing the development of the master teacher. Since the teacher-student ratio offers a concrete measure, it has rapidly become a popular demand. Even families from the lowest income groups have become aware of and concerned with these ratios in their own schools.

[1] Lawrence A. Cremins, *The Transformation of the School: Progression in American Education* (New York: Alfred A. Knopf, Inc., 1961), 21.

As mentioned earlier, there is a mass of evidence that the size of class or the individual teacher-pupil ratio is not a crucial point of entrance for transforming the slum school. There are obviously desirable upper limits, but the mechanical allocation of new resources to reduction in class size does not produce significant increases in educational effectiveness. In fact, concern with class size has the consequence of fixing on existing practices of classroom management and can operate as a barrier to real innovation.

Closely related to the emphasis on reduction of classroom size in the specialization model has been the growth of specialist personnel in curriculum matters, and also for discipline and counseling. Efforts to upgrade the college preparatory programs and to utilize the development in the cognitive theory of curriculum construction have led to the introduction of specialists whose task it is to assist the teachers and supply them with technical support. The development began in suburban college-oriented systems and has spread in varying degree to the large city school systems.

In support of the curriculum specialists are those university-based groups that prepare materials incorporating scientific and intellectual developments. These curriculum teams have been heavily subsidized by the Federal government. It is generally recognized that the materials these groups have produced have markedly raised the academic content of high school, and as mentioned above, are part of the contemporary trend to assign to high school an important aspect of undergraduate collegiate instruction.

Nevertheless, it needs to be pointed out that individual authors have rapidly entered the field of new mathematics, new biology, etc., with the result that high school textbook preparation also continues in its traditional format since there are many stylistic advantages to a book written by a single person or two authors. The important development is not government-sponsored team-work in curriculum development but rather the shifting of se-lected subjects from the collegiate level to the secondary school. Moreover, these national curriculum efforts have had little rele-vance for the problems of the slum school; and in fact, by increas-ing the specialization of the suburban high school in college prep-aration, they have weakened the comprehensive high school and worked against the needs of the youngster of the inner city.

But limitations in the curriculum development movement emerge most pointedly in the actual day-to-day work of the curric-ulum specialist in the inner city school system. Their work, like the new materials, is again oriented mainly toward the college-bound student who can benefit from accelerated instruction, and not so much to the marginal college student who needs remedial or supplementary work. The curriculum specialist is typically con-cerned with subject-matter issues rather than fundamental is-sues of student instruction in academic and vocation programs. He is not concerned with classroom climate and he does not usu-ally develop stable and effective relations with classroom teachers. Subdued tension often results when the teacher sees him as an-other unrelated specialist with whom she has to come to terms. The impact of the curriculum specialist has been, in general, to weaken further the authority and self-respect of classroom teach-ers rather than to serve as an effective resource for them.

By contrast, the aggregation model does not emphasize class-room size per se, nor the introduction of an independent hier-archy of curriculum specialists. Instead, the aggregation model is concerned with improvement in the overall management of the classroom and in increasing the professional authority and pro-fessional autonomy of the teacher. The teacher accepts the re-sponsibility for managing all that goes on in the classroom and for coordinating the relations between the classroom and the family as well as other community contacts. Therefore, it is not in error to speak of the teacher as the teacher-manager, since she has at her disposal a variety of nonprofessionals plus outside assistance which can be utilized at her initiative. The teacher-manager seeks to prevent the classroom from becoming detached and isolated from the rest of the school and the larger community.

Emphasis is on organizational flexibility and away from fixed standards of classroom size. The goals are toward organizing a series of daily and weekly educational experiences in which the ratio of instructional personnel (and their qualifications) vary from one educational task to another. Involvement, particularly in musical, cultural, and social science presentations, can be in large auditoriums led by master teachers, while in the course of each week, each student can receive individual homework help from paid high school students. The teaching of history and geography can proceed in normal size classes, while there can be no effective reading program in a slum school without small group activities, augmented by individual tutorial instruction. These practices have existed informally under superior teachers in a single classroom; the objective is to institutionalize them and make them part of the total school program.

The aggregation model emphasizes not only the variation in the size of learning groups but also the transformation of the classroom situation to eliminate the solo-practitioner approach of the specialization model. As discussed below, teacher aides, volunteers, and personnel supplied by Vista and the National Teacher Corps become members of a team under the teacher-manager and are able to develop an effective sense of cohesion and enhance the position of the teacher.

Curriculum specialists under such an arrangement are not part of an external hierarchy, but resources that can be utilized at the request of the teacher. The teacher-manager becomes a focal resource for in-service training that is designed to assist new personnel entering the slum school. The principal finds himself not directing a group of relatively isolated teachers, but rather supporting and coordinating the work of an aggregation of teaching teams.

The teaching team seeks explicitly to face the grim realities of the disorganized slum and its negativism toward education. Instead of semi-annual grading, a continuous development format is more appropriate to deal with the high degree of residential mobility found in the slum community. It makes little sense to conduct an educational system in which a great many fail regularly. The continuous development system is designed to overcome repeated and pointless failure without denying the realities of the students' limited levels of achievement.[2]

The continuous education approach is designed to break out of the rigid track system that engulfs the slum school. Basically, the youngster is permitted to proceed through the curriculum at a speed compatible with his intellectual capacity. It is recognized that he will have different aptitudes in various subjects and his rate of progress will vary accordingly. Research has demonstrated that the continuous education system is not only a technique for organizing the curriculum into manageable segments, but if effectively implemented it is a much broader strategy which results in changes in classroom management embodying elements of the aggregation model.[3] Fundamentally it brings the teacher into much closer contact with the pupils, and helps develop a more collegial relation among teachers and between teachers and supervisors.

Under the traditional format, slum children are graded at most

[2] See Mary A. Queeley, "Nongrading in an Urban Slum School," in David Street (ed.), *Innovation in Mass Education* (New York: John Wiley & Sons, 1969).

[3] *Ibid.*

semi-annually and passed or failed for a whole year's work. The system operates with the norm being failure; by the time youngsters enter the third grade, the bulk have either failed or retardation in achievement is becoming pronounced. Under the continuous education system, the curriculum is organized into much smaller segments. Grading and evaluation is done each month or each six weeks. The child is not permitted to pass on to a new level until some effort is made to help him master his present level. He is not required to redo the same materials since alternative materials can be offered. Research results indicate that the continuous educational program not only produces short-term overall improvements in performance, but also that the teacher knows more about the children and the attitudes of the students toward the teacher and the school are improved.

Since continuous education permits progress at different rates, the student can make use of his different abilities. This is especially important for boys in slum schools who seem able to perform much more adequately in mathematics than in reading. In addition, the continuous education method fits with the social life of the slum with its high residential mobility, since students who move in a school during the academic year can be placed in their appropriate level of achievement with greater facility.

Classroom management means improvement in the capacity of the teacher to deal with discipline and disruption within the classroom setting. There are sufficient data to underscore the fact that in the slum school the teacher spends most of her time on such matters. In the specialization model, discipline problems are assigned to specialists in interpersonal relations and to the adjustment teacher or assistant principal for discipline. Although the decision to suspend or expel must be made by an official other than the classroom teacher (but under more effective due process), the aggregation model broadens the role of the classroom

teacher and increases her competence in controlling deviant behavior.

A central dimension in maintaining freedom and order in the
classroom is the teacher's expectation. Hostility is generated
among the students not only on the basis of covert prejudice—
racial and social class—which must abound given the differences
in social backgrounds and experiences of teachers and students.
To recruit teachers from the Negro community does not eliminate this problem. Hostility is also generated when teaching personnel devalue the human worth of their students, operate on a
narrow definition of achievement, or underestimate their students' capacity for personal and intellectual growth. These negative definitions, although hardly verbalized, are rapidly communi-
cated and contribute to the opposition culture of the slum school.
Self-scrutiny, including staff group discussions where the teaching personnel can openly talk about their fears and attitudes and
formulate new standards of performance for the slum school are
essential. Under such an approach the personnel in charge of discipline shift their focus from merely administering negative sanc-
tions to serving as focal points of in-service training.

AUTHORITY AND DECENTRALIZATION

Because piecemeal programs of innovation have failed to produce markedly more effective schools, there have emerged widespread demands to transform the authority system of the inner
city school system. Citizen groups became concerned with plans
to "decentralize the school system" or to widen the "participation
of citizen groups" in making decisions. When these demands are
pressed by Black Power groups, frustrated by the lack of progress
over the last decade, they develop explosive overtones.

The demands for decentralization and citizen participation, in
addition to their realistic elements, have become ideological slo-

gans, that is, goals desirable in and of themselves. Decentralization, in particular, is only an organizational strategy that can be justified if it changes the behavior of principals and classroom teachers and of parents as well. Decentralization serves societal goals if it makes it possible for inner city schools to render more effective and more individualized services.

A basic problem of the inner city school system, however, is that it has become detached from the suburban school system in terms of its financial base, its personnel practices, and its fundamental social relations. Any system of decentralization that serves to maintain or reenforce such separation can hardly be judged as making a positive contribution. Thus, from the point of view of equality of resources and strategic goals, greater centralization, or at least more uniformity of objectives, is required while decentralization of operation is being sought.

It is also necessary to recall the earlier discussion of the institutional realities of the inner city school system. Mechanical and arbitrary plans for decentralization cannot be effectively fused onto an organization that is highly fragmented. School decentralization runs the risk of contributing further to internal disorganization; in some respects increased centralization is required. In the simplest terms centralization and decentralization need to be judged both in terms of (a) fundamental policies and goals and (b) specific and operational practices. Thus, a case can be made that important aspects of public education need to be more centralized in order to guarantee a greater equality of resources, while other aspects such as curriculum development require effective decentralization.

The issues of authority and decentralization are debated in terms of the number of operational units that should come under one jurisdiction and the appropriate number of levels of administration. Nevertheless, alternative strategies of decentralization and citizen participation have meaning only if they actually change patterns of authority and they can be evaluated to the degree to which accountability is increased. From the point of view of the aggregation model, the transformation of authority must start from the very top of the system. Decentralization requires simultaneous, or even prior, efforts of creating an effective central managerial core. There must be enough of an integrated organization so that decentralization can be meaningful. An effective managerial core means that there is a group of appointed officials and their professional counterparts who have enough of a sense of institutional solidarity so that fundamental issues are identified and confronted or at least debated.

The first steps rest with personnel and the procedures of members of the school board, for only in rare cases do the members feel that they have penetrated into the real life of the system and exercise effective control. When they are not overawed by the personality of the superintendent, they are often overwhelmed by the complexity of the issues they must face. Various reforms have been proposed and some implemented such as developing a policy agenda which moves away from operational details by devolving these issues onto the office of the superintendent. There have been efforts to devise more adequate procedures of recruitment, screening, and even training of board members and the development of small independent staffs to serve the board with documentation, research, and planning. None of these devices have produced startling results, although the effectiveness of school boards has clearly increased in the 1960's.

It is abundantly clear that the traditional pattern in which the superintendent serves as the sole link between his system and the board of education no longer suffices, if in fact it ever did. Board members require some form of direct access to the machinery of the public school system. At least one metropolitan system follows the practice of encouraging board members to develop areas of expertise and to become part of the supervisory apparatus of particular operations. Another possibility is to institute the equivalents of the Congressional committee which would permit board members to have direct access to school officials. There is enough experience to indicate that such arrangements need not weaken the position of the superintendent. Instead the consequence of effective involvement of board members in the operation of the system can be to make them more effective spokesmen in mobilizing public support.

The second and more important set of steps rests on increasing the professional and organizational authority of the general superintendent as a precondition for effective decentralization. One key requirement is to broaden his ability to modify the structure of his central staff, to change its function, and to select his own direct aides. In the first wave of managerial change, when younger men became big city superintendents, most accepted their appointment without insisting on freedom to appoint their key aides; they were prepared to make use of existing personnel. Since 1965, some new superintendents have insisted that they be able to replace top personnel even though they may be covered by civil service or administrative decree.

The immediate objectives are to overhaul the internal division of responsibility, to simplify the top structure, and to create a central office staff equipped with modern managerial resources and management techniques such as electronic data processing, performance budgeting and fiscal control, etc. But the underlying objective, more difficult to achieve, is to transform the central staff from an operating agency seeking to administer the details of a large and complex system into a planning, controlling, auditing, and coordinating agency. In city after city, steps have been taken to relieve the superintendent of detailed and routine tasks and to free him for organization development and representation to the public. Following the pattern of industrial management, which in turn is based on the format of the military agency, one key officer, in effect a chief of staff, is appointed as understudy to the superintendent, charged with the management of the central staff. But it has been a slow task for transforming the activities of the central staff away from day-to-day functional activities. Much of the development of the resources of the central staff has been consumed in obtaining, processing, and administering Federal funds.

Paradoxically, the development of a chief executive officer has not facilitated the transformation of the central staff, for this format operates effectively in a relatively stable organization which is not continually facing crises. But each of the inner city school systems of the United States is straining to transform itself. The central staff reacts to external pressure and crises; it continues to perform the operational oversight of day-to-day function and the chief executive officer is more likely to be an administrative expediter who has an essential but limited function of giving the superintendent some additional assistance. Examination of the operating format of six of the big city systems reveals that innovations at the top take place, not because of the development of a "rational" organization format, but almost in spite of it. If there is a key administrator who is dedicated to changing it, tension is a sign of progress.

The basic ingredient for innovation is the assumption of the role of "associate superintendent" for innovation by one officer who may be called planning officer, or research and development officer, or just special projects officer, and whose work cuts across that of the chief executive officer and the various functional chiefs. He is a person who has the support of the superintendent and who is prepared to penetrate into the internal mechanism of the organization. He is, so to speak, the officer in charge of modifying the organization, not of administering it. Although such a set-up does not appear to be an adequate permanent arrangement, it serves immediate requirements and is likely to persist. If the central staff emerges as a planning and coordinating agency, its effective organization will in turn become more of a council-type or a planning team of different skill specialists. Under such circumstances, the principal executive officer becomes the chief planner and the operational lines of authority descend from the board of education to the general superintendent to the chief operating superintendents.

Over the short run, however, with the creation of a more effective central staff, the conditions are created for initial steps toward effective decentralization of particular administrative procedures. Operational decentralization can lead to the conception of the McGeorge Bundy report that was offered in 1967 as a remedy for the New York City system where a partial system of decentralization had had limited effects.[4] The goal is to create the smallest possible operational unit, to give each the maximum amount of autonomy, and to broaden citizen participation drastically by creating many more local boards. The plan recommended some sixty to seventy distinct local school units. In a sense, each unit is seen as becoming a specialized agency created to meet the particular needs of a local area and developing as far as possible a distinct character. Such a plan raised a wide range of questions. Does such a system contribute to overcoming the fractionalization of public education and the professional isolation of teachers and principal? Does it enhance lateral communication between operating units and internal communication within a given school? Does such a system make possible economies of scale in

[4] *The New York Times,* November 8, 1967, p. 1, col. 1.

routinized functions? Does such a plan create the necessary conditions for an effective career service? Although these questions are difficult to answer, this effort to decentralize and to increase citizen participation appears to maintain and enhance an excessively fractionalized system, and in fact, the original plan was modified by city officials in order to meet such criticisms.

An alternative effort at decentralization proceeds in the opposite direction by dividing the central city school system into three to seven superdistricts or sectors, each of which becomes the top operating agency. In each sector there is a relative balance of the social composition of the inner city. In Chicago, for example, three sectors with associate superintendents were organized at the same time that the Bundy report was issued. The superintendent of each sector seeks to make use of those economies of scale that can be achieved. But the establishment of the sectors is designed to increase organizational effectiveness by (a) narrowing the span of control, (b) increasing lateral communications among operating units, and (c) most important, increasing the organizational authority of the individual principal.

For the moment, the crucial question of the number of operating units that are appropriately linked together under a middle level of administration (the district superintendent) will be postponed for discussion below under the topic of pupil composition and decentralization. If a decentralization program has impact, however, it is because there is first a change in the behavior and performance of the individual principal. Two dimensions are crucial: First, to expand the range of the decisions that a principal can make; increase his role in recruitment and selection of personnel, broaden the authority he has to reallocate the resources placed at his disposal, increase his authority to make arrangements for community groups, including the recruitment of volunteer and paraprofessional, and enhance his authority to modify curriculum and make him and his staff responsible for decisions concerned with which specialized training and special work programs youngsters are to be offered. The number of years of school and the requirement of school attendance and performance should ultimately not be based on mechanical citywide norms, but the judgment of local school officials and their staff. Second, the relation of the principal to his teachers and his students needs to change. The principal cannot be an administrative agent; he must represent and personify the teaching function. He must be the principal-teacher in the school.

All of this was well known to the traditional principal who sought to make himself effective throughout the school by his sheer physical presence and his direct involvement in the daily routine of the teachers and students. Under the aggregation model, the principal must retain his teaching function, although the content of this function will vary from situation to situation. This is not to assert that he engages in teaching on only a token and symbolic basis. The analogy with the medical hospital has some relevance. The principal is required to perform like the chief of a service; he is the doctor among the doctors, so the principal is a teacher among teachers. This may mean that he operates as the chief in-service training officer for his staff, that he is engaged in classroom teaching, or that he is directly available to parents and students as well as outside community leaders. He has at his disposal an administrative assistant, a chief clerk, who manages the routine administrative tasks and who is part of an administrative career service that allows for promotion and increased responsibility via a career route to larger schools or to higher levels of administration.

The objective of effective decentralization is to guarantee a public presence within the school and thereby increase the likelihood that the public school system will render effective services to each student. Parent or community participation at the level of the district or individual public school is designed to be precisely such a device. Outside groups such as volunteers and members of the Teachers Corps also serve in the same fashion. They are mechanisms of accountability. Parent involvement in slum areas, even if it is based on local leadership and not merely a reflection of organized outside professional or church leadership, can have defects and limitations. For example, one occasional result is an increase in parental pressure for punitive disciplinary school authorities. Moreover, it is generally recognized that local boards are at a disadvantage in assembling specific and technical information in comparison with the advantages that accrue to the permanent professional staff. A decentralized school board system would be strengthened if it has recourse to an *ombudsman* system, with full-time civil servant personnel to process grievances.

But insuring an effective public presence in a slum school requires more than an *ombudsman* system. A public presence is enhanced if personnel involved are not limited to investigative functions but have positive duties as well. Thus the presence of Vista workers, volunteers in the schools, and other school groups serve both the positive goals of supplying important services to youngsters, and an informal grievance system.

In the United States the public school has resisted an effective internal audit and inspection system. In England and in the other Commonwealth countries, the school inspector is a standard administrative agent for insuring a public presence and in strengthening equality of service.[5] The British inspectorate is both a system for checking on performance and the adequacy of administration and instruction, and at the same time a device for helping and supporting the classroom teacher and the local administrator.

[5] E. L. Edmonds, *The School Inspector* (London: Routledge and Kegan Paul, 1962).

The inspectors are drawn from classroom teachers and local administrators. They are personnel who have demonstrated their high competence in educational pursuits, and their loyalty to the educational system. They are, however, required to represent the needs of parents as well as checking on the performance of teachers and local administrators.

In the United States, the educational profession has succeeded in preventing an internal inspection system. Even the military have a highly developed inspector general cadre. There can be no effective transformation of the public school of the inner city without the development of some such equivalent agency. In terms of the aggregation model, it is most likely to be meaningful if it has the multiple function of representing the public interest and at the same time helping teaching personnel in dealing with operational problems and serving as a channel of communication from the operating level to supervisory levels.

PUPIL COMPOSITION AND SCHOOL BOUNDARIES

Decentralization involves not only the professional authority of the principal and of the teacher but also basic questions of student composition and school boundaries. The traditional comprehensive high school was an informal decentralized education system because different social classes were educated within one school. When the comprehensive high school operated effectively, it served the dual need of offering a common social experience plus a differentiated curriculum. The school made its contribution to a common culture and at the same time enabled lower-class students to participate in a college preparatory education. Not all youngsters attended effective comprehensive high schools but enough did so that the school system operated on a basis compatible with the assumptions of the larger society. With the growth of urban centers, specialized academic high schools were introduced but even these did not Europeanize public education because of the citywide recruitment. Moreover, attendance at a purely academic high school was not the exclusive route to higher education.

Since 1945, the comprehensive high school in the central city has declined because of limited financial resources and because of the patterns of population concentration, particularly of lower-class Negro families. Given the fragmented organization of public education, the quality of education in a particular school is deeply and immediately influenced by the population characteristics of the community. Therefore, the task facing the aggregation model is to organize school boundaries and student populations so as to produce heterogeneous social backgrounds, including racial integration. It is relatively easy to reject the approach of Robert Havighurst to reorganize the public school system so as to achieve racial integration at the expense of maintaining or even sharpening social class differences.[6] But the effort to develop alternative strategies has produced much writing and little consensus.

The problem is profoundly complicated by the fact that efforts at integration have been in the ring of primary and secondary schools that are located on the edge of the Negro ghetto. These areas are, with some notable exceptions, the least equipped and have the most limited social resources for handling the impact of school integration. Programs for school integration have tended to involve low-income Negro and white youngsters or whites of lower income than their Negro counterparts. Racial integration in education can proceed more quickly among better educated groups especially in communities with concentrations of professional families where the Negro and white youngsters are of similar middle-class background and where the quality of public education is good.

Since the 1954 Supreme Court decision, school integration in

[6] *Op. cit.*

the minds of the public school administrator and in the public perspective has been cast in formal and numerical terms and on an all-or-nothing basis. In a given school building a student body should be made up of an admixture of Negroes and whites who need to share a common educational experience during the whole day, the whole week, the whole school year, and throughout the pupils' entire schooling.

School integration can also be seen as an aspect of the larger social process, however. If the task of school integration is to make it possible for the Negro to enter the mainstream of American society, school integration becomes, in one sense, a reality whenever there are cross-racial contacts for pupils. The movement toward integration takes place when these contacts occur— for one hour, for one day, for one week, or for an occasional semester. The same desirable consequences take place when youngsters—both Negro and white—have fuller exposure to an integrated group of teachers. The conception of social process integration is not limited to an "all-or-none" outlook but includes the utilization of a range of opportunities.

There is also a psychological dimension in the concept of school racial integration that has grown in tremendous importance since the issue was first pressed by Negro groups and the Supreme Court decision of 1954; namely, that of self-respect and identity. The requirements of the Negro youngster cannot be met by the assumption that only by attending a white school can good education be achieved. There must be effective education in all Negro schools if Negro youngsters and the Negro community are not to be locked into a position of psychological inferiority. Already in 1963, Bettelheim and Janowitz anticipated the implication of the rise of the Black Power movement. They argued that school busing and other devices could not suffice to incorporate the Negro into the educational mainstream. They pointed out that for some youngsters, moving into a white school, although better in facilities, teachers, and educational content, would of necessity result in lower self-esteem or continued low self-esteem.[7] It would reenforce the notion that Negroes are a deficient group for whom special arrangements must be made. In this sense, the cultural separatism of Negro groups can be seen as an alternate search for self-esteem.

In a parallel fashion, the notion of a heterogeneous social-class population requires a conceptual clarification. Public discussion of this issue was for a period dominated by the findings of the Coleman report which concluded that the composition—that is, an appropriate mixture of social classes (or racial groups)—is the single most powerful indicator of educational performance.[8] For purposes of the aggregation model, let it be assumed that the Coleman findings are adequate although there is reason to question many particular conclusions.[9] Therefore, massive integration, both social and racial, is required, and many sociologists have recommended the wholesale "breaking up" of the slum school by massive busing, the building of vast educational parks, and the relocation of public schools outside of the inner city. In time, James Coleman himself declared his reservation on this point of view as being the major or overriding implication of his research.[10]

Reasonable objection to an exclusive massive social integra-

[7] Bruno Bettelheim and Morris Janowitz, *Social Change and Prejudice* (New York: Free Press, 1964), 93–95.

[8] James S. Coleman, *Equality of Educational Opportunity*, Office of Education, U.S. Department of Health, Education and Welfare (Washington, D.C.: Government Printing Office, 1966).

[9] For a critical evaluation of the limitations of the findings of the Coleman Report, see Samuel Bowles and Henry M. Levin, "The Determinants of Scholastic Achievements—An Appraisal of Some Recent Evidence," *The Journal of Human Resources*, 3 (Winter, 1968), 3–24.

[10] James S. Coleman, "Equal Schools or Equal Students?" *The Public Interest*, 4 (Summer, 1966), 70–75.

tion formula rests not on moral judgments. Nor is the central reservation politically feasible. The difficulty with the approach is that it accepts the existing criteria of school success as the basis for according respect and even employment opportunities to the Negro. It accepts the given school system when in fact a great variety of changes are required for both whites and Negroes. Fundamentally, regardless of the importance of a single factor, it is a gross error to assume that only this factor can and needs to be altered. Even if social composition is the single most powerful variable, it is the responsibility of the social scientist to specify the conditions under which effective and quality education can be achieved by alternative methods.

Thus, in terms of the aggregation model, the quality of the education program in a particular school need not be thought of as simply a reflection of the social composition of the student population, although it is obviously deeply influenced by it. If the inner city schools are to become more of a social system, and less fragmented, programs and personnel become as important as modifying the social composition of the student population.

If the comprehensive high school is to be adapted to the needs of contemporary social structure, at least two dimensions are involved in the aggregation model: First, no pupil should attend a high school which does not have a college preparatory program. The number of pupils in the high school need not be a limiting factor. Of course, it can be recognized that the scope and quality of college programs are likely to vary. But if an essential element is absent in a particular high school, it could be obtained by attendance during the academic year or for a given time period at a central facility. Equally important is the presence of continuous devices for insuring and encouraging transfers into college preparatory programs. Second, no youngster should be required to attend a high school that is organized around some particular technical or vocational program. Again, for specific training and for specific periods of time a student may attend a specialized vocational training center or community facility, but his basic education program involves participation in some form of a comprehensive high school.

Thus the two requirements of concern with racial integration and social-class heterogeneity (plus a relevant diversity of educational programs) converge and lead away from a concern with single boundaries to multiple boundaries depending on the program involved. At the high school level, in fact, boundaries are de-emphasized and the concern is with effective centers.[11]

The checklist of basic steps to maximize racial integration are by now well known. They are implemented not because of the concrete results they achieve; they are demonstrations of the commitment of the public school authorities to reasoned pursuit of the objectives of integration. These policies include citywide open enrollment to utilize unused school space and to enhance racial balance. Devices for managing integration include selected busing and community programs to retain white families. Demonstrations of social process school integration include mutual exchanges of pupils and teachers with suburban communities from periods of one day to one week or even one semester. But the main thrust of pragmatic integration focuses on the maintenance and development of a set of key comprehensive schools—magnet schools as they might be called—in which attendance is based on a sector or even on citywide basis. Realistically, the maintenance of a number of such magnet schools is still a goal in most of the major metropolitan centers of the United States.

For such schools, and more generally, fixed purpose buildings

[11] There is an interesting analogy between the national community and the educational community. Edward Shils speaks of the center and the periphery as elements in a nation, and in the same fashion an educational community requires both. See Edward Shils, "Centre and Periphery," *The Logic of Personal Knowledge—Essays in Honor of Michael Polanyi* (London: Routledge and Kegan Paul, 1961), 117–131.

need to give way to more multipurpose centers that can be adapted to changing educational needs and changing age populations. In urban renewal areas, where the maximum amount of integration has taken place, and also in model cities programs, it has become possible for physical school planning to be more adequately related to community housing programs. Flexible school buildings do not have to be invariably publicly constructed or publicly owned. Instead particular structures can be leased; some can even be built as parts of housing developments and thereby be financed by alternative schemes to bonds authorized by popular elections. When grammar schools are built by private developers and leased to the public school, Federal mortgage insurance is possible and the costs are less because the school system is not involved in capital costs. But in any building program there is no need for a magnet high school enrollment to be larger than five or six thousand to insure the necessary variety of educational programs.

School integration under the aggregation model also involves sound planning of housing. The South Commons housing development on the near South Side of Chicago represents one model of the combined efforts of the private sector and the Board of Education to attract middle-income families with school-age children into a racially integrated setting. Selected inner city communities continue to serve as desirable residential communities because of their access to business institutions as well as cultural and social facilities. The basic question is whether these areas will be rebuilt for families without children—either young and newly married families, or families that are returning to the central city after having reared their children.

High concentrations of apartment house structures serving specific age groups without school-age children cannot be viewed as contributing to a viable social fabric. In addition to controlled density and a heterogeneous social-class composition the vitality of the metropolitan community is served by more balanced age groupings. To achieve these objectives integrated social planning of housing and school are required.

After World War II, a section of the near South Side of Chicago, then called Douglas Park and just south of the Loop, underwent massive land clearance. This formerly elite area had become a slum with the majority of the dwelling units beyond rehabilitation. In retrospect, it could be argued that clearance should have been more selective. But it has also been argued that only such a concerned effort in the 1950's could have produced racially integrated housing at that point in the history of American urban communities. And in fact on this cleared land, some of the earliest large-scale interracial housing projects in the United States were started —Lake Meadows and Prairie Shores. Although there was some concern for public schools, the basic strategy was to appeal to families without children or with preschool children by means of middle-income high-rise construction.

In the early 1960's the remaining portions of the cleared land in the Douglas Park area, directly east of Prairie Shores and Lake Meadows (in the vicinity of 28th Street and Indiana Avenue) were offered for community development. There was good reason to follow the existing pattern with additional high-rise structures which, because of the access to the Loop, would extend the scope of interracial housing in the city of Chicago.

Nevertheless, the additional goal of creating a housing pattern that would serve families was clearly an objective of the local community and of the City Council. Members of the Center for Social Organization Studies, of the University of Chicago, assisted private developers in creating a plan with this goal which was submitted to the Department of Urban Renewal and accepted by the City Council of Chicago. In contrast to the uniform high-rise pat-

tern of Prairie Shores and Lake Meadows, the physical structures contained a mixed pattern. They included high-rise structures, low-rise buildings, double-level duplexes, and single-family
row houses. The plan called for 1,400 units and a population of
4,000 persons.

The key element was the social planning, which included provi-
sion for a community building including a church and a public
school, constructed at the expense of the developer. The schools
in the immediate area were all Negro, and it was anticipated that
even white families committed to integrated housing would not
accept such school facilities. It was necessary to draw the original
plan without the involvement of the authorities from the Board of
Education. As the construction was started a mutually acceptable
approach was fashioned by the Board of Education, and local
community groups, including representatives from the adjoining
public housing complex served by a single nearby public school,
the Drake School. The school in the South Commons development
would be leased to the Board of Education and this facility would
be administered as a regular public school. The Board of Education guaranteed that this facility would be integrated thereby re-
moving a barrier to new residents to the South Commons project. It
was also a long-term objective to develop an integrated school in
the underutilized Drake School which was all Negro at the time of
the planning in 1968.

A step-by-step program was projected. Initially, the South Commons school will conduct grades kindergarten through four, with
additional multigrade facilities as required. These will be the
grades that will be required if families are to be attracted to South
Commons in the first phase. Since the projected ratio of families
was estimated to be 70 per cent white and 30 per cent Negro, integration in the South Commons education facility can be assured.

Additional youngsters from the Drake School will complete the student body to the extent compatible with acceptable integration standards. There will be one principal and a common name for the new school—The South Common/Drake School. As the pool of white students increases and as they move through the upper grade levels, the South Commons facility and the Drake facility will be run on a jointly integrated basis, one serving the lower grade levels and the other the upper grades. The end result, it is anticipated, will be not only a racially integrated school but also one with a range of social backgrounds of the students in attendance. As part of the program in both schools, special efforts are being made to develop quality education appropriate for an integrated community.

Each metropolitan area requires realistic goals of the numbers of students that will in a particular time period be involved in a magnet type of high school or will attend other types of integrated schools. The purpose of these goals is to remind the educators of the scope and nature of the problems facing students who do not attend such settings. Thus, the aggregation model asserts that the effectiveness of the slum school is increased primarily by changes in its structure and personnel—rather than mainly by manipulating its student composition. Decentralization and flexible boundaries are part of a strategy of reconstruction from the top down—from the central administration core to the individual school, and from the higher grades to the lower grades.

Finally, the need for flexible attendance areas does not mean that the district level of administration, the level between the operating school and the large sector, can be entirely eliminated. The number of districts needs to be reduced so that each sector will probably supervise five or six districts. The district level, aside from performing housekeeping functions such as maintenance, etc., emerges more as a focal point for teacher education and professional in-service development.

TEACHER EDUCATION AND CAREER LINES

Professional education and in-service training for teachers and administrators cannot be separated from their career lines in public schools. Just as teacher education and in-service training are being refashioned, so too has there been a recasting of the format of educational careers. The specialization model, representing a conscious and deliberate effort at managing educational institutions, has had its greatest impact on the education of teachers and principals. The specialization model is a creature of professors of education and they have been able to make themselves felt. And, in turn, strangely enough, important counter-trends against the assumptions of the specialization model can be seen in the steps taken in the last decade to modify teacher education. Very little has been accomplished to alter career lines, however, for these issues are embedded in administrative decree and public law.

Under the specialization model, the school of education developed as a distinct and specialized institution to train personnel. Professionalization meant specialization. Schools of education separated themselves from the main body of substantive and intellectual life of the university campus. They prepared not only teachers for public service but also, more important, future professors of education for teachers' colleges and state universities. Both in the schools of education at universities and teachers' colleges, the emphasis was on the methodology of teaching. These institutions also were able to develop a near-monopoly position in advanced training for educational administration. In most states advanced degrees become essential elements for promotion and a substitute for in-service training. All of this is painfully well known, and the strong reaction has led to powerful and widespread efforts to broaden the educational background and deepen its content for prospective teachers and to provide them with more of a general education and additional substantive knowledge in their area of primary interest. Teacher education has moved gradually in a direction which is at least compatible with the notion of the teacher as a manager, if a proper system of clinical and in-service training existed.

But the central problematic issue is whether the training of teachers should be further removed from colleges and universities and given over to the public education school system. The obvious weakness of schools of education and teachers' colleges in their clinical staff argues in this direction. They have a marked absence of cadres of professionals with outstanding classroom teaching experience; that is, men and women who continue to perform as teachers and therefore set models for the new generation. Previous teaching experience is not sufficient. The clinical professor of education is a person currently engaged in teaching and in supervising teacher training. The organization of the school of education is markedly different from that of the medical school where the clinical professor is a key element in the professional training of medical students. But such an approach still leaves unsolved the form, timing, and content of such professional education. The most important argument in favor of continuing to involve schools of education in professional training is that these schools are committed to educational research. Deep involvement in clinical and professional training is essential to enrich and invigorate their research efforts, which have at times been described as excessively detached from educational realities, especially those of the inner city.

More important than the locus of professional training is its essential content and format. Under the specialization model the crucial experience was the practice-teaching experience. Basically, students in education were exposed directly and suddenly to a classroom full of youngsters. It was a kind of trial by fire. It was an experience of professional shock, like exposing the medical student to the human cadaver. There was little effective preparation for the assignment and very limited on-the-job supervision and training. The prospective teacher was supposed to succeed or fail. This method worked in a period in which there were more applicants than jobs. It was a particular experience which was relatively separate from the academic preparation of the future teacher. This approach was and still is consistent with the specialization model.

To the extent that there has been a change in the professional aspects of teacher education, the strategy has been to build a bridge between academic instruction and clinical practice teaching. Academic work in the social sciences is both an element of liberal education and an experience designed to prepare the student for the realities of the classroom. Social science instruction involves not only reading texts—more often textbooks than original texts—but also direct observation of small groups in classroom situations and participation in a variety of community settings. Without explicit doctrine, there has been a growth in the basic notion that practice-teaching starts with a variety of individual-to-individual experience (one-to-one) or small-group experience rather than with the direct plunge into the full classroom. There is a process of aggregating different social involvements before becoming a practice-teacher. Thus, the teacher in training engages in community and social work, participates in youth activities, assists with homework help, and does reading or storytelling with small groups.

Each of these experiences of a teacher in training becomes the basis of group discussion and supervision. In preparation, the practice-teacher is given an opportunity to observe a variety of classroom teachers before he starts his own work. Practice-teaching involves supervision by a master teacher and forms the basis for staff conference-type courses of instruction. The practice is another ingredient in converting the classroom from a closed, isolated, and detached setting to a more open and integrated element of a larger system.

Under the specialized model, the teacher received training in a specialized college of education, was exposed to a single period of practice-teaching, and obtained more advanced instruction by returning to a school of education for a master's degree. Entrance into the administrative post required advanced degrees from such institutions. Under the aggregation model professional education is balanced by greater exposure to in-service training. Advanced formal education is seen as part of general professional education for teachers and administrators, but professional development rests on in-service training. Moreover, in-service training becomes an essential element in the restructuring of relations between teachers. In-service training is designed to improve lateral communication among teachers and supervisors and to improve collegial relations—in short, to convert teachers from isolated solo practitioners to groups of professional peers with a high degree of social cohesion.

In-service training fuses with the tasks of internal administration and curriculum development. The forms of in-service training are various, but the content draws heavily on the critical exchange of on-the-job experiences, personal success and failure. In-service training thus becomes a device for institutionalizing individual innovation. The accomplishments of the gifted teacher can be disseminated through staff conferences in the immediate school setting, or special training institutes.

Career development in turn is broadened and made more flexible. Experiences in community and welfare work during teacher training which were designed to improve the competence of the classroom teacher-manager can continue after certification. It has long been recognized that ex-social workers often make effective classroom teachers in slum communities and job rotation in this direction is possible for the classroom teacher. Teacher-managers have the opportunity to assume for different periods community-oriented tasks; they can, in fact, become school community agents and again return to the classroom.

But there is an additional and crucial aspect in career development. Recruitment into a principalship under the specialization model is a decisive step that places the person in a new and distinct career from which there is no turning back. Under the aggregation model, although the bulk of the principals would be committed to an administrative career, the career development system permits movement out of the administration back into classroom teaching, especially into the role of master teacher. The consequences are greater flexibility in individual careers and a better matching of responsibilities and aptitudes at differing points in the life history of the educator. It becomes an honorable solution for those who find administration unrewarding or who are unable to adapt to administrative pressures. At the higher level of administration, career flexibility implies lateral movement from one system to another, rotation of job specialization, and even opportunity for sabbatical employment outside of the public school system.

NONPROFESSIONALS AND VOLUNTEERS

Both models seek to make use of nonprofessionals (or teacher aides) and volunteers. Because of the emphasis of labor intensive methods, the aggregation model, in contrast to the specialization model, gives greater weight to the importance of such personnel.

The aggregation model also implies a greater number of such personnel, a wider range of sources of recruitment, and a broader scope of their involvement. The specialization model emphasizes the use of nonprofessionals in administrative and housekeeping tasks. Their work may extend into borderline educational tasks such as working in the library or assisting in field trips. But the aggregation model, while seeking to make use of aides and volunteers in such roles, also includes their direct participation in educational activities.

Under this approach teacher aides and volunteers participate in educational tasks mainly by tutorial work, either with small groups of youngsters or on a one-to-one basis, and thereby offer children additional academic assistance. The underlying strategy is not merely an intensification of the same type of effort made by the classroom teacher. To the contrary, small-group work and tutorial assistance is a form of supplementary help which the teacher is unable to offer. These nonprofessionals can offer their attention and their energy to establish satisfactory and stable relations with youngsters. They can seek to find a common ground and to supply a sense of immediate gratification to the youngster as he struggles to improve his academic achievement. The rewards for improved academic achievement are too remote to be a powerful incentive to many youngsters in slum schools. The immediate acceptance and encouragement that these additional personnel can offer is at the basis of improved performance.

The teacher aide or the volunteer can serve the limited but crucial role of homework helper and thereby extend to a lower-class child the type of support that middle-class parents normally give their children. The teacher aide and the volunteer worker can also assume more direct involvement in small-group work, such as reading groups, or special work in particular subject-matter areas. The most elaborate and direct involvement, which is still feasible for untrained but supervised personnel, is in one-to-one tutorial work in reading, arithmetic, and other basic skills.[12] Careful research with adequate control demonstrates the effectiveness of volunteer workers in helping lower-income children to improve reading skills.[13] These researchers also report on the impact of such efforts on orientation toward school, general interpersonal adjustment, and indicate measurable, if limited, positive consequences.

Nevertheless, the incorporation of teacher aides and volunteer workers into the public school system has proceeded very slowly during the last decade. Organizational rigidities, formal requirements, opposition from professional groups and trade unions, have served to confine their utilization. It has often been the case that a large public school system will institute programs in order to demonstrate its interest in innovation, without developing appropriate administrative support to enable them to expand in numbers or have an important impact on the school system. Only in a few cases have vigorous public school programs been encountered in large metropolitan centers where the need is most pressing. Paradoxically, suburban areas and smaller communities have some of the most effective programs.

As a result, a great deal of energy in the innovative uses of nonprofessionals has been displayed outside of the public school system. Strong impetus for the use of volunteers was given by the efforts of college student groups linked to the civil rights movement in the early 1960's. These efforts, which received extensive

[12] See Gayle Janowitz, *Helping Hands: Volunteer Work in Education* (Chicago: University of Chicago Press, 1965), for a description of the various educational roles that nonprofessionals can perform.

[13] Richard Cloward, "Studies in Tutoring," *Journal of Experimental Education,* 36 (Fall, 1967), 14–25; Gayle Janowitz, "After-School Study Centers: Experimental Materials and Clinical Research," Center for Social Organization Studies, University of Chicago, Chicago, Ill., 1968.

mass media coverage, helped to dramatize the role of the volunteer. However transitory the nature of many of these student organizations, changing student interests and excessive publicity brought about a decline of these programs. Funds from the Office of Economic Opportunity have also supplied important resources from out-of-school or after-school centers. Particular programs, such as Mobilization for Youth, in a bold fashion made use of local high school students as paid tutors. Throughout the country selected church groups, settlement houses, and social welfare and youth service organizations have launched educational and cultural enrichment programs that require nonprofessionals and volunteers. The performance and stability of these efforts have been varied and essentially depend on the quality of the supervision of volunteer personnel.[14] Often, the uncertainty in Federal funding procedure disrupted these efforts. And these programs become institutionalized in time and in many urban centers citywide coordinating and supervising groups have emerged to give them stability. Thus, there is reason to believe that the future of nonprofessionals in education is likely to involve both in-school and out-of-school efforts.

The development of nonprofessional and volunteer programs in the public school system depends on more effective decentralization. Steps to recruit and select teacher aides and volunteers are often linked to the existing central personnel offices. Application to be a teacher's aide requires a visit to a central office or, at best, to one of several key offices. In addition, teacher aides are generally seen as full-time posts. Both of these requirements serve to limit the number of available personnel and the effectiveness of these programs. The aggregation model seeks direct recruitment of local

[14] Timothy Leggatt, "After School Study Centers: An Analysis of a New Institution," Working Paper No. 51, Center for Social Organization Studies, University of Chicago, Chicago, Ill., November, 1965.

personnel; and this is enhanced if selection can be in the hands of the local principal. The need for effective decentralized arrangements in the recruitment and allocation of volunteers is even more important. Citywide volunteer bureaus are important, since a great deal of the personnel who serve as volunteers come from outside the immediate area of the school in which they serve. But the principal needs to have flexibility in making direct arrangements with individual volunteers and with groups of volunteers.

Excessive concern about adequate selection of such personnel is often a subtle but effective technique for limiting these programs. The needs of the slum school are so great that some risks are worth taking, and experience indicates that the problem of unfit personnel is not a significant one. Some simple screening procedures are required, but these programs develop more effectively if the emphasis is on supervision and on-the-job training rather than on selection or pre-service training. Ineffective or undesirable personnel can easily be terminated if they fail on the job or they can be counseled into other jobs that they can perform.

Under the aggregation model, the emphasis is not on recruiting a stable force of teacher aides and volunteers, although this is a desirable objective. The nonprofessional and the volunteer, especially if they are high school students, are being exposed to experiences that have educational and socialization value for them as well as for the youngsters they are serving. It is also recognized that the nonprofessional and volunteer may have experiences that will influence their career decisions, mobilizing them to seek additional training. Such programs become important devices for recruiting a new generation of teachers. Teacher aide programs that utilize local personnel serve to resocialize into the larger community women who through childrearing, especially under the conditions of the slum community, had become almost wholly detached and preoccupied. In the most basic terms, the slum school is built in a community of high birth rates and therefore one of great imbalance in young people as compared with older persons. The use of nonprofessionals and volunteers in school and in after-school study centers represents an effort to create a social climate with a better balance of age groups. Local adults who become involved in such programs have an opportunity to interact with adults outside of the narrow range of their immediate family and social group.

THE IMPACT OF THE NEW MEDIA

A core issue in educational innovation is the actual and potential use of the new media in education. The term "new media" has come to mean the massive and expensive instruments of television and the machinery of programed learning. It is also important to include the new technology of the little instruments, such as tape recorders, film strips, and the family of technological developments for duplicating printed materials, from inexpensive paperback books to more efficient duplicating machines for classroom use. The professional autonomy of the teacher-manager depends on the type of investments that will be made in the new media and on the organizational control for using them. The new media force the administrator to be concerned with investments that can be either labor intensive or capital intensive.

In general, the potentialities of the new media for improving educational effectiveness have been overemphasized. But educational institutions can no longer operate without these devices. Because the United States is a technological society, there has been and will continue to be strong pressure to introduce these devices as rapidly as possible and on a most extensive scale. In the last decade, considerable resources and administrative energy have been used to introduce the new media into public education. The utilization of these media can be analyzed in terms of the differing requirements of the specialization and the aggregation models. The effectiveness of these media is not exclusively determined by their technological form, but is also deeply influenced by the conscious decisions of educational administrators, as to how they have to be organized and used. The actual experience with educational television in contrast with paperback books supplies a paired comparison since television has been employed in a format which conforms primarily to the specialization model, while paperbacks —more by accident than by design—have reflected the outlines of the aggregation model.

In the early 1950's, under the stimulus of the Ford Foundation, extensive steps were taken to develop a national network of local transmitters for educational broadcasting. One result of this system, contrary to original expectation, was not a device for classroom instruction but rather a telecasting system for general audiences emphasizing popular culture and aimed at adult populations. Continued interest in classroom television led to a variety of experiments in metropolitan closed-circuit television and to an elaborate system of airborne educational telecasting in the Midwest. The airborne system had to be abandoned because of its inefficiencies and rigidities. The result was that classroom television never developed the role that its advocates anticipated. The use of television was based on a highly centralized format in order to obtain the maximum economic benefits. A group of media specialists who were concerned with the technical problem of presentation and who were distinct from educators managed these enterprises. There developed sharp antagonisms between the media specialists and the subject-matter personnel. In fact, television was introduced by an organization operating initially outside the school system. As a result, despite economic pressure to use television, educational television has failed to gain widespread acceptance. Television is just another specialized and unarticulated resource. Instead, one of the main emphases of educational television has been to develop a national network of outlets which broadcast to the general audience and serve to enrich the content of programs available to the adult population.

One basic limitation in the use of classroom television is its lack of flexibility—that is, its lack of adaptability to meet varying classroom needs. The more centralized its control, the more inflexible are its uses. Because of the limitations on "feedback" and interaction with the instructor the system has profound limits. Teachers resist television because of the loss of autonomy over context and scheduling when it is introduced. But it was the highly centralized format under which television was introduced, more than its inherent limitations, that accounted for its limited development.

Nevertheless, it is possible to identify the format under which television can be adapted to the aggregation model. The educational power of television is the sense of immediacy that it can impart. It is particularly relevant for presenting the raw materials of the humanities and the social sciences. It is less relevant for teaching specific skills and specific technical content. For science instruction, television can project demonstrations and experiments rather than regularized instruction. Interestingly enough, experience has indicated that closed-circuit television can be used as an effective medium for communicating with teachers and assisting them in the preparation of their classroom instruction. Thus it appears that television needs to be utilized at a scale less than its maximum coverage if it is to fit into the school system. Moreover, the proposition needs to be explored that, paradoxically, the better the student is academically, the more he is able to benefit from the special experience that television can offer.

By contrast to the disjunctive and limited force of educational television, the spread of inexpensive paperback books has had a great impact and has conformed much more to the aggregation model. The new paperbacks are essentially an economic matter, cheaper per unit cost and having greater flexibility of content. They have improved the professional autonomy of the classroom teacher and greatly increased the diversification of the curriculum. At all levels, the teacher has more control of the curriculum because books can be produced and distributed more cheaply. From a technological point of view, the new printing processes could have made for greater standardization of curriculum materials. But, to the contrary, the organization of production and the systems of selection of these materials has meant both an upgrading of content and a greater role of the classroom teacher in developing the curriculum.[15] First, the new technology has meant that the needs of specialized audiences can now be served on an economic basis. Special editions of the classics and of original materials can be produced in appropriate quantities to serve relatively limited needs. Distribution companies have developed that have penetrated the public school system so that diversified libraries are available in high schools that never had adequate hardback facilities. It is true that such libraries have been slow to develop in slum schools, but there are enough examples to show that they can succeed in serving students of such schools. *Hooked on Books* is a report of the successful use of paperback books in an education program in a Michigan correctional institution and a powerful demonstration of the ready audience for literature among the so-called culturally deprived.[16]

---

[15] Thomas S. Smith, C. T. Husbands, and David Street, "Pupil Mobility and I.Q. Scores in the Urban Slum: A Policy Perspective," in David Street (ed.), *Innovation in Mass Education* (New York: John Wiley & Sons, 1969).

[16] Daniel Fader and Elton B. McNeil, *Hooked on Books: Program and Proof* (New York: G. P. Putnam's Sons, 1968).

Second, the economics of paperbacks is such that more and more school units can afford to augment basic texts with specialized and high-grade printed materials. Third, and more fundamental, the book publishing industry is highly decentralized and very competitive. For both hardback and paperback texts, most big publishers are forced to offer more than one title to teachers. The impact of this competition has been to weaken the authority of central curriculum selection committees, and to force them to allow their teachers to select from a wider variety of titles. It is now very difficult for a public school system arbitrarily to designate a single basic text and argue the necessity of this text on the basis of economic advantage. This is not to claim that there is sufficient decentralization in curriculum construction, but that the books in the new media format are being used with increasing flexibility and professional discretion.

Improved duplicating and photocopying machines serve to decentralize further the production and control of printed media. The classroom teacher can enter more actively and directly into the production of materials. Outstanding teachers have traditionally prepared their own materials. Such materials not only can be tailored to particular interests and aspirations of the class, but also have the attraction of conveying the teacher's personal involvement. These new media enhance the teacher's ability to produce such documents. There is reason to believe that the unit costs for certain formats are no higher than more centralized materials if all costs are included. As an abundance of case materials underscore, the fullest decentralization of curriculum construction and the maximum involvement, particularly for the slum school, come when the students themselves produce by dictation or composition their own reading materials, and these are duplicated for use by their peers.

The consequences of the new media will probably be duplicated in the application of computerized program instruction. With these capital intensive devices, as with television, there is an initial tendency to exaggerate the potential impact. This is especially the case for low-income youngsters, for whom interpersonal processes in learning are so crucial. Nevertheless, there does exist some latitude in introducing and managing them so as to make them compatible with the requirements of the aggregation model.

The bulk of computerized learning equipment has been initially introduced at the college level. From a public policy point of view these funds might have been more justifiably spent to broaden equality of educational opportunity. College students, who have successfully internalized the norms of independent study, are probably better equipped to deal with computerized program learning equipment. If there is a role for such equipment in the inner city school, the hypothesis is offered that it will be for those who are best equipped and most strongly motivated, while for the bulk of the youngsters the basic processes of education will have to emphasize labor intensive techniques.

Thus, if the new media are thought of as including more than high-cost television, there is every reason to believe that they can be used to strengthen and achieve the goals of the aggregation model. Good educational results are not directly related to the costs of the resources required.

5. School-Community Relations

In order to give content to the specialization and aggregation models, the term "school-community relations" has to be given a delimited scope. It encompasses much less than the locus of the school in the national social structure and the broad consequences of education on the society. School-community relations involve the immediate contacts of the school with individual families—complete or broken as the case may be—and with organized groups that penetrate into the immediate neighborhood. Of course, school-community relations extend to include those patterns of communications that link the central staff with the city as a whole. In this sense, school-community relations have direct ramifications on national institutions, but the specific purpose of the concept is to highlight the linkages of the school and the community at the micro or local level.

In its local contacts, the slum school by comparison with the suburban school was a relatively closed institution. Up until the recent past, boundaries of the slum school and the outside community were fixed and sharp, as well as difficult to penetrate. If parent-teacher groups in middle-class or suburban areas have been judged to have limited influence and effectiveness, the tradition of the slum school has been one of ephemeral parent organizations. A considerable minority had no organizations and in many schools the leaders were selected in effect by school administrators. Their effective function was to suppress conflict and limit contact. Their programs were infrequent and limited to perfunctory official announcements and ceremonial functions. Only rarely was the parent organization used as a device for implementing the education programs of the slum school.

The typical pattern of contact with an individual family or parent has been essentially negative and even on occasion repressive. Direct day-to-day observation underlined the consistent pattern by which the public school in the slum community operated to keep parents from understanding its educational program. Parents had to live with a lack of adequate information and with much misinformation about school procedures and the obligations of the school authorities toward their students. Inquiries by parents were generally discouraged by arbitrarily limiting office hours, by rude and officious behavior toward parents, and by creating a climate in which youngsters inhibited their parents from making inquiries since they had come to believe that such inquiries would "make trouble" for them. School authorities took the initiative when they wished and this was mainly on the occasion of pronounced misbehavior.

The "horror" stories that circulated were not exaggerations or isolated cases but reflected operating procedures. The bulk of parents were unaware of the names of the teachers and never had contact with them. Children could be arbitrarily suspended from school for periods of many months without any recourse of appeal. Even when new programs were initiated they were frequently created arbitrarily, without regard for the realities and pressures of family life. The fact that as late as 1968 the Chicago Board of Education still resisted listing the telephone numbers of its local schools is perhaps an apt summary of the accumulated traditions.

Social-class barriers and racial prejudice were certainly at work since professionals prefer contacts with persons of their own

background. Again and again, in observing the impact of experimental programs financed by poverty funds, principals and teachers were noted as much more polite and responsible to middle-
class personnel on these projects and to middle-class volunteers
than to the parents of the local youngsters. It is even reported that
professionals behaved differently to parents and to volunteers on
the same occasion. The impact of the civil rights movement and
the pressure of black associations has meant that public school
personnel must spend more time on these matters, especially in
dealing with organized groups. But the resistance to change in
dealing with individual parents is very powerful and school professionals retain considerable ability to limit contact and communication. Basically, the slum school officials, because of their defensive posture, see the intrusions from the outside as potentially
disruptive.

Decentralization of authority and deemphasis of geographical
boundaries set the conditions for transforming the slum school
into a more open institution. With the increased demands of civil
rights movements and Black Power groups, organized relations
between local school officials and community groups have taken
a wide variety of forms. At one extreme are those isolated but
persistent situations of outright struggle between community
groups and the local school which lead to boycotts, strife, and
various forms of coercion. Short of such "warfare" are those situations where the tactics of pressure, or merely personal antag-
onism, inhibit change and block a flexible response by school
officials. Nevertheless, even in the absence of systematic research, one is struck by the fact that frequently in slum communities the quality of contacts between local school officials and
organized community groups is very fluid so that patterns of
mutual accommodation often arise rapidly from situations of
conflict and hostility.

With the exception of specific situations where militant groups are able to mobilize a "confrontation," the quality of school-community relations is not primarily fashioned by such group representations since at best only a very small proportion of the slum community makes use of these channels. As described above, there is a network of personal communications, images, and rumors out of which the substance of school-community relations are built. At the root are the operating policies of each school which function with a very different set of assumptions from those that reflect the social and cultural conditions of the slum.

The basic idea that youngsters should be separated by grade runs counter to the social organization of the slum family where kinship and the conglomeration of brothers and sisters and relatives are the organizing principles of survival. (One of the reasons for the success of after-school study centers is their willingness to recruit and accommodate kinship groups rather than age groups.) The time schedule of the public school is fixed and likewise at variance with the tempo of the slum community. There is little effort to serve children who come early to school and equally limited effort to operate flexible after-school and evening programs.

The basic notion of the summer vacation hardly articulates with the life style of the slum. Except for changes in temperature, there is little special about the vacation periods. As vacation time approaches, the youngsters of a slum school, especially those in the primary grades, become restless and even more difficult to handle, for they are fully aware that the limited element of structure and stability in their lives is about to be disrupted. It may well be that restructuring of the format and time schedule of the school is the first and indispensable step to altering school-community relations.

The aggregation model stresses the need for enlisting the family in specific and concrete support of the school's educational program. The school must be prepared to face indifference of parents, but modest efforts have been observed to produce noteworthy results. The requirements laid down on the families must be very realistic, such as helping to establish a homework time, adequate scheduling of meals, and insuring basic care of books and supplies. Parents must be encouraged to visit and communicate with the school personnel on a freer and more informal basis.

Energetic principals and teacher-managers can change parental attitudes by creating the conditions in which parents can make a contribution to the life of the school. Some of the hostility of parents to slum schools rests on their recognition that the teaching staff thinks of them as incompetent and ineffective in helping to educate their youngsters. But each parent can make a meaningful contribution to his own child. In the conduct of the school, if there is a wide and flexible range of activities, parents can accompany children on field trips or furnish food for social events. A measure of the success of community relations is the extent to which slum families develop enough of a positive commitment to a particular school to alter their tragic patterns of short and frequent residential movement, a form of mobility that has been demonstrated as thwarting academic achievement of their youngsters.[1]

The specialization and the aggregation models indicate different strategies in broadening school-community relations. The specialization model seeks to make progress by adding a specialist to the staff of the local school, the school-community agent. Such a person frequently has a background in community affairs or is given training in community organization. His task is to facilitate communication between the school and both organized group interests and individual families. This development represents

[1] Smith, Husbands, and Street, *op. cit.*

an important step in that it gives the professional staff another device for communicating specific messages and its point of view to the families of the students. It serves also as a reverse channel of information.

School-community agents are often appointed without a clear definition of their job. This is of limited consequence since their role must of necessity be diffuse. They also rapidly accumulate specific tasks and become involved in concrete tasks of social welfare, family referral, and the like. At times tension develops between the school-community agent and the school's officer for discipline affairs since the school-community agent assumes the more "therapeutic" orientation. Out of such tensions, however, a clearer recognition of the conflicts between the values of the school and of the community emerges.

For the aggregation model, the task of school-community agent is a natural extension of the teacher-manager's responsibility for his pupils. The school-community agent and his indigenous assistants are deeply involved in family and community welfare problems, especially for the youngster at the early age level. But the community agent under the aggregation model is centrally involved in the educational process because it is assumed that the goal is that each youngster must have a meaningful role in the local community. For the bulk of youngsters in the slum school, the formal academic and vocational programs alone are not able to afford sufficient gratifications to be an adequate basis for self-esteem and a moral order. If students have to remain under educational supervision until sixteen, school experiences must be fused with community or work experiences. Therefore two basic elements are involved. First, the aggregation model seeks to permit youngsters to pursue educational and cultural experiences outside of the school. Second, the youngsters' educational development involves participation in satisfactory work experience in addition to community recreational and cultural activities.

The school community agent is active in overseeing those educational and work experiences of each student that take place outside of the school. Again and again, for reasons that are only dimly perceived, youngsters will find in an outside educational program involvement and satisfaction that they cannot develop in a school setting. Success in an outside academic program can, over time, dampen negative attitudes toward the school. The existence of educational field stations in the community are indispensable as second-chance agencies.

In the past, public school systems have been hostile to other institutions and agencies that have offered educational work—church groups, community organizations, settlement houses, and welfare agencies. Until recently, the school has almost purposefully separated itself from these agencies and at times has been openly antagonistic to them. Under the aggregation model, the school is more supportive of outside agencies with educational programs. To make the school and the classroom a coordinating locus does not mean that the school is the sole center for learning. The tragedy of the slum is not only its physical deprivation, but also the anti-humanistic values that it fosters and maintains. Not until youngsters feel that outside of school they are more able to read or do their homework or participate in musical or cultural programs with ease can it be said that the aggregation model has been achieved.

Thus, the school system must take the initiative to insure that a variety of facilities are available in the community for the slum students to do their homework, pursue musical and cultural activities, and form associations based on these interests. The settlement house traditionally had an educational function in assisting the foreign born; contemporary community agencies are gradually returning to this tradition. The after-school study center—maintained by a church group, a youth or community agency—has emerged as a new device for pursuing this goal. Improvement of school programs in slum areas is not likely to eliminate the demands for such outside community resources but to increase their importance and use.

The expansion of opportunities for work experiences is central and it involves a positive role by the Federal government. Such schemes must involve new opportunities within ghetto areas or very close to them. It must rest on a variety of tax incentives and investment schemes, the analysis of which rests outside of this paper. Nevertheless, many of the families in the slum community would require support by some form of negative income tax, and whatever earnings derived from the activities of their youngsters cannot be used to reduce family income. From the point of view of the reconstruction of the climate of the school, the allocation of these training opportunities must be oriented toward rewarding those students who actually and positively contribute to a school system based on mutual respect rather than on coercion. This does not mean that over the short run or in a crisis situation gang leaders cannot be co-opted, but that long-term strategies must be designed to change the basic informal leadership.

The following are illustrative examples of the range and type of work experience that are needed. School-directed efforts might involve as much as 75 per cent of the student body in particular areas:

1. For the 5 or 10 per cent of students who are the most successful academically, there are paid educational tasks, such as those of homework helpers.

2. For a group of about 20 per cent, varying degrees of specialized training in vocation centers on a part-time or part-year basis are available. These youngsters are subsidized to a limited extent, such as for carfare and lunch. They are students who would be likely to complete school because of their commitments and motivation and because their self-esteem was high enough for them

to see the relevance of their specialized training. Their specialized training is designed to increase their employment possibilities after graduation. Moreover, such vocational and specialized training carries with it intrinsic rewards, both in the prestige it accords and in work satisfaction for it serves as a stimulus both to broader involvement in academic high school programs and in some cases to post-high school technical training.

3. For the largest group, approximately 30 per cent, part-time work experiences in the outside community with varying amounts of pay are required. These are the students with massive degrees of indifference or hostility and with great variation in motivation. They would truly be the ones paid to go to school. Generally, their work habits are poor and their skills are limited, but the range of employment opportunities must be thought of in very broad terms. This would include participation in various types of community improvement programs, working in local community and social agencies, employment in municipal agencies and commercial or retail establishments. In slum communities, there is a pressing need for homemakers, medical aides, welfare assistants, recreational workers, and tutors. The work experiences need to include these tasks for the benefit of the local community and as a way of introducing these youngsters into the labor market. It will be necessary to create within existing industrial establishments, or in new agencies, specialized employment opportunities for such youngsters—a version of sheltered workshops or a form of "good will industry."

4. For a group of about 10 per cent, regular involvement in a work program is very difficult because of their antisocial or gang type behavior. They must be involved in various forms of adventure corps or uniformed groups, such as the Boy Scouts, where a different program and reward system are involved—for example, recreational programs and group activities including shorter and

longer periods at residential camps in the country, fashioned as the civilian conservation corps—but they must maintain their basic identification with their local public school.

RECONSTRUCTION OF COMMUNITY SERVICES

In varying degrees both the specialization and the aggregation models imply that the classroom teacher become more of a focal point for the coordination of community services. But this aspect is more stressed in the aggregation approach. In turn, the requirements of the public school become a central focus for articulating programs of economic and social development in the local community. With the passage of the Model Cities Act of 1966, national policy clearly recognized that the structure of housing, welfare, medical and mental health agencies was no longer appropriate for dealing with the conditions of life of the inner cities, that is, if it ever was. In order to make better use of existing and increased public expenditures, the objective of greater citizen participation was enacted into law. Of equal importance is the necessity for a conceptual transformation in community services similar to the alternative models of change in public education offered in this essay. These dimensions are much more diffuse and are not readily reducible to holistic concepts. Nevertheless, for institution building in the inner city schools to proceed on a comprehensive basis, professional educators must be aware of and involved in alternative strategies of community development.

Two issues are illustrative of the types of reconstruction that are required to assist the operations of the public school system. First is the separate, detached, and isolated pattern of public and private agencies which render particular services to slum residents and which produce the so-called referral system. The policy issues center on the alternative strategies of consolidation of these agencies which have an external and separate resource base. The persistent question is the articulation of the local community with the large society. The second issue is on the other end of the social spectrum. The issue is the articulation of the housing pattern with the social and economic needs of the individual family. The policy issue is how to reduce the vulnerability of the low-income family by altering its immediate housing pattern so as to make possible a better linkage between the family and the public school system.

As in the case of educational innovation over the last decade, a variety of segmental reform programs have been undertaken throughout the United States. There have been experiments in the use of nonprofessionals in social welfare and community work; new types of mental health clinics have been organized and in particular considerable progress has been made in family planning in low-income areas. The amount of systematic evaluation which has been undertaken in these experiments is even more limited than on the segmental innovations in mass education. It does appear that beneficial results have been obtained. In the absence of a fundamental restructuring of the welfare community services system, however, these particular achievements are hardly dramatic or drastic.

If one makes the assumption that new forms of guaranteed annual wages are to replace the older welfare and aid to dependent children payments—issues which must be resolved at the state and national level—it then becomes possible to examine the component elements at the community levels of the first issue, the structure of agency services, and the second, the patterns of housing, as they impinge on the public school. In both cases the Model Cities Act of 1966 creates legislative pressure for drastic social experimentation and more rational social planning.

First, the diffuse structure of service agencies—welfare, medical, recreational, housing, and legal—results in the separation of the private and the public sectors and the existence of local, state, and national hierarchies of each. Each hierarchy has an independent existence and therefore operates at the local neighborhood and community level as a separate and distinct unit. The division of labor between these agencies is the result of historical accident without essential rationale, and the sources of funding and vested interests maintain these separately. In the simplest terminology, they are organized for the convenience of the professional producers and not the clients (the consumer). In the minds of residents, there is no basis for understanding their jurisdictions since they are not organized along functional or problem lines. As a result there has emerged an elaborate system of referrals by which persons are shifted from agency to agency; in general, their office hours hardly articulate with the needs of the local residents.

The weakness of the structure of local welfare, health, and community organizations has been recognized for over thirty years, but the political conditions for change have not developed. The system is more than inefficient. Because of the excessive referrals and the inability of any specific agency to demonstrate adequate responsibility, the residents develop strong hostility and resentment. Segmental change has led to a stress on creating city-wide welfare councils and local interagency groups or devices for improving the referral system and increasing coordination. The residents must come to deal with a greater variety of agencies whose specific functions hardly match their problems. They have to face numerous bodies whose task it is not to render service but to refer and coordinate. Thus in the near North Side community of Chicago in 1962, when a comprehensive effort on social planning was launched in connection with the Delinquency Control Act of 1961, it was found that for a population of sixty thousand residents there were two separate coordinating councils for over fifty agencies, including areas which were mainly referral points. In fact, all that was absent was a formal organization for coordinating the two local coordinating councils, although there were informal mechanisms for this purpose.

The tensions that are generated produce intense political conflict as local militant groups attack "welfare colonialism," and demand "local self-determination." The struggle leads to direct efforts to gain control over political party groups, but more often the local party structure is bypassed as community groups press for direct access to governmental agencies. In general, each outburst and new power balance are followed by efforts at accommodation with the existing agencies since local leaders who assume power are quick to learn the limitations of self-help and the necessity of technical assistance and resources from the outside community.

Because the restructuring of parent and operating agencies, both public and private, is a slow and difficult process, one strategy is to develop a new type of community center in which the local representatives of the various service agencies are to be found in a single physical structure. By physical consolidation, steps could be taken to develop a more rational division of labor and a fusion of responsibility to the residents. At this community center there would be those personnel who are able to render assistance. It would be a single stop "supermarket" without the confusion and rigidity of a referral system, and it would be operated like a hospital on a continuous-day basis.

A model for one community on the South Side of Chicago, for example, projects a medical facility as the central unit, but in this building would be found the welfare agency, family service and legal assistance, and an employment unit. This consolidated agency would serve the area of a school district. The artificial barriers between agencies would be weakened and deemphasized.

Crucial to its effectiveness would be a continuous twenty-four-hour schedule and extensive telephone assistance. From the point of view of the aggregation model the single central referral depot would facilitate the tasks of the classroom teacher and the school community agent. This approach requires the construction of a central building facility or the conversion of an existing facility to this specific purpose. In essence, the purpose is to create a focal point where residents can obtain information and assistance without regard to the existing organization of agencies, but in response to persistent problems that require resources from outside the community.

With regard to the second issue, the strengthening of family life and its articulation with the school environment, one strategy focuses on housing arrangements. National policy of massive concentration of low-income and welfare families, the majority of whom are incomplete families, has been a failure, although in a relative sense it represented a clear improvement in the conditions of life. Given the goals of contemporary American society, the standards of performance of these complexes are below those acceptable both to the residents and to the larger society. The emerging phase includes such different approaches as the construction of scattered-site housing, home and apartment ownership for low-income groups, or the use of rent supplements so that families can rent in the open housing market. Again, the objective of a guaranteed annual wage is an essential element in these efforts to give families greater control over the conditions of their housing.

Nevertheless, if the objective is an individual housing space that would throw each low-income family on its own resources without adequate physical facilities for community support, the results are likely to be self-defeating. To reject the massive housing project hardly implies that detached single-family units are the desirable or possible goal for the inner city. The self-contained and detached family life space of the middle-class image has its profound vulnerabilities. But it is hardly appropriate for low-income incomplete families. Family life requires a housing pattern that would facilitate a variety of types of mutual or collective support. In particular, common facilities for day care of children are of the highest importance.

Such an approach would emphasize a form of communal housing, a modified and urbanized version of the Israeli kibbutz where mutual family support is viewed as an important goal. Each family has its own self-contained life space, but there is built into the housing pattern common areas for group and multifamily activities. Common space would exist for day care of children, for recreational and educational activities, and for group festive occasions. The types of housing would be mixed, and would involve widespread rehabilitation of existing facilities. But on each floor there would be common recreational and study space, and in each building there would be common day care and educational facilities. These spaces assist mutual assistance, especially among incomplete families. In large buildings or in groups of buildings, the school, through its school community agent, would maintain an outpost and would operate as a focal point for the teacher-manager's outreach efforts. It is common to hold that the problem of the slum is not merely physical; but physical facilities are required both for the consolidation of social and community services and a more adequate setting for family contribution to educational activities.

6. Conclusion

An appropriate approach to summarizing the argument of this essay is to recall that the large city public school system—the one that serves the inner city—has been and continues to be described by many sources, professional and popular, as an institution that strongly resists innovation and directed change. There can be no doubt that the inner city school system, because it is not an articulated social system, has many elements that can be characterized in these terms. The suburban school is much more responsive to pressure for change. But to accept the global formulation that schools resist change more than any other institution in our society is in fact more harmful than useful. Over the past fifty years there has been considerable interest and effort in improving educational administration. In fact, there have been waves of change which, at worst, have produced overreaction to external pressures or superficial changes at best. The basic problem is no longer that the public school system resists change. The issues are that inner school systems do not have the capacity to plan or launch comprehensive change to deal with any particular problem or student population. Partial and segmental change has been the order of the day, with unanticipated consequences that have worked to the disadvantage of the inner city school.

In this sense the political realities and the political style of the United States has until the early 1960's meant increased inequalities in education, or at least failure to reduce those inequalities that have produced explosive political outbursts. With the rediscovery of the politics of poverty, the main instrumentality of change has been Federal aid to education. The first phases of increased Federal aid meant that new funds were allocated to meet ongoing costs. New programs were highly segmented and in fact the bulk of the experimental funds was used at the periphery of the school system, rather than as a basis of fundamental change. As of March, 1966, for example, of the $757 million that had been allocated by the Elementary and Secondary Education Act, the largest amount went into preprimary programs, and, to a lesser extent, into summer, after-school, and Saturday efforts. The decision was made again and again to add specific program elements rather than to restructure the system. There were few programs such as teacher training, model schools, school-community agents, the recruitment of teacher aides, or funds for central planning. The process of utilizing Federal funds for fundamental change is one of altering the professional perspectives of top administrators. It has been argued in this analysis that the absence of conceptual models, such as involved in the distinction between specialization and aggregation models, has been a powerful constraint.

This is not to overlook the full impact of the sociopolitical context of the inner city school and slum community. The political slogan that the slum is without adequate control over its density has been raised to assist political reform which would produce a better balance in educational resources between the suburbs and the central city. But the numerical ratios are such that the political change becomes more difficult. For the first time in United States history, the majority has to modify its position of privilege, rather than the traditional pattern of requiring a minority to compromise.

On the other hand, Negro cultural separatism simplifies the process of social change. The social definition of effective education in the inner city has proceeded since 1954 in terms of the desirability of an integrated racial pattern. Only an occasional educator would point out that even the most ambitious plans for racial integration would leave large numbers untouched and that effective education has to be achieved in all-Negro schools as well.

The rapid rise of black cultural separatism in 1967 dramatically and suddenly transformed the political setting for debating segregation and integration in American society and public education and there is no longer any single social definition of desirable social change. A more pluralistic outlook has emerged. The analogy with ethnic relations after World War II is most pointed, although it must be clearly recognized that ethnic relations in the United States are fundamentally different than race relations because of the harsher realities of segregation and the deeper levels of prejudice, yet the analogy is still revealing.

Until World War II, the dominant notion was that of the melting pot; namely, that all foreign-born groups would gradually disappear and their particular cultures would be eliminated and a common American culture would emerge. This was the trend and it was a desirable outcome for a democracy that needed only to be assisted. After World War II, however, the notion of "beyond the melting pot" began to replace this social goal. Although ethnic ties were weakening in the United States, they were persisting to a much greater extent than had been anticipated. To some degree they were reenforced by the new migration. Although the numbers were small in comparison with older waves, they included many professionals and intellectuals who were determined carriers of ethnic values.

More important, the third generations of young adults were starting to rediscover their genealogy and ethnic heritage. In some cases it was a continuation of family traditions, while for others it had ideological overtones of criticism of contemporary social values. In still other cases, it was an incomplete search for identity that was strengthened by foreign travel and the study of languages and cultural history. But this was not an isolated process. The search for group solidarity involved various forms of religious participation and fused with the ethnic affiliations. It was an aspect of family and community social life.

There is no need to overemphasize the strength or capacity for survival of ethnic or ethnic-religious affiliations. They do not lead in the United States to demands for political separatism although they help maintain an ethnic vote. For large numbers they have no relevance at all; for others they are no more than a vague sentiment. In its extreme form such affiliations lead to an interest in parochial schooling, after-school instruction, or summer camps with cultural and religious overtones. It is compatible with participation in the occupational structure of modern industrialism. It is not based on submission to traditional authority, but involves a degree of choice and internalization of cultural values. It is a search for self-expression and group solidarity in a highly mobile society. The new concept of ethnic relations "beyond the melting pot" means a greater element of pluralism in the ideology of the United States and thereby a greater capacity to handle social and political issues in a heterogeneous society.

It may well be that the cultural separatism of the Negro and the emphasis on an Afro-American content represents an equivalent phase. The emphasis on integration can be equated to the earlier emphasis on assimilation which gives way to a culturalism. Like other ethnic affiliations, the degree of attachment to Negro cultural separatism will vary greatly. Some segments will develop strong commitments while others will be indifferent or hostile and will continue to press for integration. Clearly the visibility of the Negro will influence this process and the outcome will depend to a considerable extent on the social definitions of the majority group. There are and will be strong elements of strain in Negro separatism, especially if it should serve to weaken political institutions. But the new phase introduces a greater element of pluralism in American society, and in particular has the potential for making the management of the public school system a more manageable task.

It will be easier to accommodate to and meet the more pluralistic demands of Negroes. The goals of the aggregation model with full-time and part-time integration as well as effective education in Negro schools becomes politically feasible. In short, a number of formats and combinations are required and are more feasible. A fully integrated high school can have a strong Afro-American club in a middle-size city with a limited Negro population. The Negro equivalent of the Calvert House or the Hillel is feasible, not only for universities and colleges but for high school groups as well. Likewise, an all-Negro high school can have a continuous exchange program with a suburban all-white high school. Negro cultural separatism carries the risks of further fragmentation of public education, but it is also a basis of a new pluralism and a basis of solidarity.

Moreover, the goals of the school system must confront basic notions of American social values, especially those concerning social mobility. The American school system is adapted to facilitating the mobility of individuals rather than dealing with problems of group mobility. In any advanced society, the school system focuses on individual mobility and the American is but an intensification of such a trend. Higher levels of performance in the inner city must of necessity mean increased ability to prepare individuals as individuals for entrance into the occupational structure. But the contemporary requirements of social progress mean that the school system must also become concerned with group mobility, that is, with the transformation of the slum as a social entity. Again, it needs to be stated that group mobility depends, of course, on fundamental social change, such as the introduction of the negative income tax and the elimination of outmoded systems of social welfare. But to the extent that the school system is concerned with socialization, and with its normative climate and with the immediate self-respect of the student, it is involved with issues of great mobility.

The application of the specialization and the aggregation models have focused on the specifics of inner city education, and on Negro youngsters in particular. While the inner city school system serves primarily the Negro, it is obvious that there are other groups for whom this model has relevance—Spanish speaking groups, southern migrants, and pockets of offspring of older European immigrant families. There are also the inadequately educated segments in suburban areas who attend school districts which, although small in size, have many of the characteristics of the inner city.

But the notion of the aggregation model is relevant to the entire social structure. In suburban areas, the "crisis" in public education presents an equivalent disarticulation between the academic goals and socialization goals. The growth of hostility toward educational authority and the patterns of personal disorganization derive from an overemphasis in high school on narrower and narrower criteria of test achievement, from a prolongation and uninterrupted period of higher education, as well as from a separation of the life experiences of the school from the community. In particular, the aggregation model should serve to produce a more integrated and varied educational experience and should help blend school with nonschool experience, through community service and work service in a fashion most compatible to the needs of the inner city.

For the inner city, however, the basic implications of the specialization and the aggregation models rest on political issues of Federal versus state and local control. On first glance it appears that the contemporary trends are toward a more and more Federalized system. The infusion of Federal funds set the conditions for such trends. But with great speed, limits on Federal intervention appear to have been reached. Devices to set standards, such as the Federal demonstration school, were rejected by Congress. The power of local political groups and the state educational offices have demonstrated their capacity to retain local autonomy.

Moreover, the issues of Federal intervention are joined with those concerning the boundaries of public and private activities in education. Because of the criticism of inner city public education, proposals to widen the private sector have emerged. In the most extreme form, parents would be given vouchers and permitted to select from public and private educational institutions according to their preference. Other approaches involve independent or private nonprofit and even profit-making established educational establishments, with both academic and vocational programs subsidized by various funds. Alternative models would include the conversion of the public school system into a public corporation, as is being suggested for the Post Office, but this does not seem to offer a basis for change. Perhaps the most powerful pressure toward increasing the private sector, or at least modifying current arrangements, is the growing feeling that only by such an approach could increased productivity be achieved, particularly because of the growth of constraints by the trade union movement in education.

In the American scene various forms of compromise are likely to emerge. Increased Federal involvement may lead to more uniform national standards of performance and more emphasis on minimum levels of performance and thereby continue to greater equality of opportunity. But the drive toward broader private sectors means an increased differentiation in public education systems. The conceptual issues of the specialization and aggregation models are drawn with the view to be relevant to differing forms of control.

Index